i

CHARLES F. FOSTER and ERIC L. JONES

The Fabric of Society and how it creates wealth

Wealth distribution and wealth creation in Europe 1000 - 1800

ARLEY HALL PRESS

Published 2013 by
Arley Hall Press
Northwich Cheshire
CW9 6NA

ISBN 978-0-9518382-5-9

This is the fifth book by Charles F Foster published by the Arley Hall Press. This book, and the previous four (1992-2004) can be bought directly from Arley Hall Press, Northwich, Cheshire CW9 6NA by sending a cheque or by phone 01565 777231 with a card, or on www.arleyhallarchives.co.uk by Pay Pal. This website features over 6000 scans of original receipted invoices 1750-90 from a wide variety of businesses which supplied Arley – the family, the house, the farms, the mills etc. These are all fully indexed and searchable.

	UK	Europe airmail rest of world surface	Rest of world airmail
	£	£	£
Four Cheshire Townships in the 18th Century	3.00	5.00	8.00
Cheshire Cheese & Farming in the North West in the 17th & 18th Centuries	3.00	5.00	8.00
Seven Households: Life in Cheshire and Lancashire 1582-1774	5.00	7.50	13.00
Capital and Innovation	5.00	9.00	16.00
The Fabric of Society and how it creates wealth	7.00	10.00	13.00

All prices include postage.

E book   ISBN 978-0-9518382-6-6
The Fabric of Society also appears on the above website as a pdf and can be read or downloaded from there for free.

I'm most grateful to my wife, Jane, for her assistance in producing this book.

Printed and bound by CPI Group (UK) Ltd, Croydon, CR0 4YY

Contents

Part I. North and South: the build-up to the Industrial Revolution in England

Eric L. Jones and Charles F. Foster

Part II. Wealth distribution and wealth creation in societies manufacturing cotton in Europe - Italy, Germany, Lancashire and Holland 1100 - 1780

Charles F. Foster

List of Figures

List of Maps

List of Tables

Author's acknowledgements and thanks

Many people have helped me create the essay in Part II and the main argument in it over the last seven or eight years and I would like to thank them all. The knowledge and skills of the following people have been particularly important: A. Antonovics, F. Crouzet, R. Hudson, E.L Jones, C.B. Phillips, B. Pullan and T. Scott. B. and P. Diaz kindly decoded the 'Wisconsin' Florentine Catasto of 1427. Eric Jones has summarised many of the results of his work in *Locating the Industrial Revolution*, 2010 (Singapore).

General Introduction

This book primarily expands Charles Foster's four earlier books. Those books provided a fairly complete picture of the social and economic development between 1500 and 1780 of an area of north Cheshire. The significance of this was that this area, just south of the River Mersey connecting Manchester to Liverpool, was approximately in the centre of the area in north-west England where the Industrial Revolution began in the 1770s. Those books all depended heavily on the marvellously detailed archives left by Sir Peter Warburton, 4th Baronet, who owned the Arley Estate from 1743 to 1774. Many of these archives have been published for the first time on the Arley Hall Archives website. The adjoining Tabley Estate, owned by Cheshire's first great historian Sir Peter Leicester (1613 - 78), provided outstanding archives for the earlier periods.

The purpose of the present book is to compare the north-west of England with other areas in England and around Europe. In the first half Eric L. Jones has kindly co-operated with me to contrast the north-west with the south of England. He has been able to fuse his knowledge of the archives of southern agriculture and business acquired over the last fifty years with the results of my north-western studies. A working life of teaching and writing about the significance of the Industrial Revolution has enabled him to set the whole analysis in the context of the evolving academic view of the phenomenon.

In the second half I have traced the social and economic conditions in four societies which manufactured cotton cloth between 1100 and 1780 - N. Italy, Germany, Lancashire and Holland. Figures produced by Angus Maddison in 2007 estimating the GDP *per capita* of countries between 1 AD and 2003 suggest that Italy, Holland and England were, in turn, the countries most successful at generating increased wealth for their populations between 1000 and 1820. From my analysis of conditions in these countries it would appear that the ability to generate increasing wealth depended on three interlinked features. In each country a society emerged where wealth was fairly widely distributed. The reasons for this were different in each country. Perhaps the absence of a strong central political authority was one common factor. Certainly in each society plural political institutions became established and these strengthened the wider distribution of wealth. Vigorous technical and commercial innovation then occurred which created rising wealth. This probably happened because many families had enough wealth to permit the innovators among them to experiment and establish their new ideas. But over the centuries some families were economically and politically more successful than others and the fortunes they made had the effect of concentrating the society's wealth in fewer hands. Some of the rich manipulated the political institutions so that they enjoyed both wealth and power and became oligarchs or magnates. The amount of innovation in the society declined and these societies ceased to be able to generate increasing wealth for their citizens - first in north Italy in the 15th century, then in Holland in the 18th century and finally in England in the late 19th century.

Charles F. Foster

Part I
North and South: the build-up to the Industrial Revolution in England

Eric L. Jones & Charles F. Foster

1 Introduction

This essay contends that it is more illuminating to look at the history of industrialization in England regionally rather than as a uniform national process.[1] This approach is employed not merely to justify presenting local detail but in order to use different regional experiences for understanding change in ways that blanket national treatment fails to reveal. Our study investigates two large areas, one north, one south, and highlights the way they diverged before and during the industrial period. We demonstrate that juxtaposing them shows larger and more prolonged forces at work than do standard histories of the industrial revolution, which truncate the past by neglecting to start before the mid- or late eighteenth century, ignoring the south, and placing most explanatory weight on the adoption of coal and steam power. We challenge this emphasis: the cascade of technological advances at the heart of exceptional productivity growth cannot be understood if it neglects the preceding intensity of market competition. Our study rests first on archival research into north-west England, particularly the Mersey basin in Lancashire and Cheshire.[2] Secondly, we present a southern counterpoint that refers to a dozen counties in south-central England, half of which have been considered in some depth.[3]

Envisaging England as a single unit is understandable since there were after all common elements at the national level, such as the legal system and economic policy. Single themes supposedly

---

[1] We are grateful to John Anderson, Tom Arkell, John Hartwick and Jeremy Morse for comments.
[2] Foster, 2002, and others referenced below.
[3] Jones, 2010.

referring to the whole country are often all that can be shoe-horned into university courses; geographical disaggregation is especially difficult when teaching non-native students who have not internalized the geographical peculiarities of England in their earlier years. Yet there is a cost: national averages cloud the bifurcation of north and south and overlook the market integration that permitted their emerging and complementary specializations. Even a two-fold analysis simplifies because intermediate patterns were produced by the successive stages of market growth: a more extended treatment might see each of our two regions as a bundle of subordinate districts, all evolving over time. Yet it was the north-south divide that came to predominate and is a division that is clarifying without necessarily being too simple. Each great region traded on its comparative advantage, amplifying developmental prospects all round.

The changes that led to the first industrialization included occasional positive shocks that were largely fortuitous but led to path-dependent and cumulative change. At their heart was the emergence right from the sixteenth century of a business culture, originally in the whole country and most vigorously in the south. But from the seventeenth century this culture was seduced in the south by the lifestyle of the gentry. Market opportunities redirected southern entrepreneurship to the agricultural sector and to overseas and wholesale trade, while manufacturing activities were slowly stifled or abandoned. In the north, the manufacturing and the business culture remained energetic, hence economic development in the two halves of the country started to follow separate paths.

The eventual mechanization of industry was obviously unprecedented, as well as overwhelmingly powerful. Although occurring later in many industries than is often implied by common generalizations, by previous standards it was immensely rapid. Yet powered machinery plainly did not arise out of thin air and it is the prelude of economic expansions and relocations to which we draw most attention, because this indicates the forces without which the cataract of Victorian industrialization could not have occurred.

While our analysis may seem gradualist it is so only in the sense that no tree acquires its leaves without a considerable spell in bud.

Nor is our argument couched in the customary form of a search for a single independent variable that sparked off all the others. The weight is placed on interacting, self-organizing developments, sustained by a political framework and general rule of law which (despite exceptions and confusions) may be seen in retrospect as flexible. Central to the case is the slow separation of manufacturing from homesteads and arable farming – away from small mixed farms - and the agglomeration effects that ensued when each activity became concentrated in different geographical areas. The model relies on the motive force of business competition within an increasingly integrated national market, which obliged firms to attend to cost-cutting and, together with improved transport and communications, encouraged them to concentrate in larger units and ever larger towns. Competition was responsible for this all-important concentration, which was reinforced when supportive trades and services emerged around the larger industrial groupings.

2 Rents, prices and locations

Changes starting in the late fifteenth and early sixteenth centuries prompted the economy to expand. In 1481 the courts recognized the copyhold rights held by a majority of farm occupiers, giving them security of tenure at a rent that was adjusted only at the expiry of the third of the copyhold's 'three lives'. Then, from about 1520, food prices rose relatively fast. The combination of a rise in product prices with fixed, or at any rate 'sticky', rents began to transfer part of the value of the land from landlord to tenant.

By 1640 rents were ten to fifteen times higher than they had been in 1500. Food prices had risen six and a half times but the wages of agricultural labourers were only two to three times higher. An underlying cause seems to have been that almost all farmland was already occupied when the population began to climb after 1500. Slow and limited though the inflation may have been by modern standards, many people had few resources by those same standards. They found it hard to resist shocks, which helped to create a new class of very poor people who had no land.[4] Social dysfunction among the landless was seen as a consequence of the inflation.[5] In 1632 the Somerset justices of the peace attributed the growing numbers of bastard children to drunkenness. By 1638 the West Riding alone contained two thousand alehouse keepers and five hundred others who brewed without licences. Puritanism was partly a reaction against the perceived collapse of morals.

For the old class of families who occupied small farms on copyhold, usually of five to forty acres, inflation brought a little windfall of capital. Their land became worth £5 to £10 per acre, whereas usually what they had to pay for it was adjusted upwards only at long intervals. The effects of the 'rent revolution' were varied. Gentry who owned estates and others with freehold land normally became significantly better off, the gains on land they farmed for themselves offsetting losses on tenanted land. But on crown land and the lands of the monasteries and church, the effect was very damaging. This was because most such land was occupied by tenants. In 1500 these three types of owner may have received 40 to 50 per cent of the annual value of the nation's land; by 1640 it was probably only 5 to 10 per cent.[6]

The redistribution of wealth affected the regions differently. For simplicity, three main zones may be distinguished rather than the two with which we will mostly be dealing: the Highland Zone (including the western side of the country), which here will be called the 'north'; the Lowland Zone (including East Anglia) which it is convenient to call the 'south'; and in addition London, which was a primate city large enough to exert an independent influence on the economy. The Highland and Lowland Zones are conventionally separated by the Tees-Exe line. They differ in terrain, climate and soils, which affect their respective production possibilities under any given technology, including new crops and methods of farming.

---

[4] Foster, 2004, pp 69 - 75.
[5] Phillips, 1999, p 376.
[6] Foster, 2004, pp 69 - 75; Allen, 1992, pp 55 - 77.

The two chief regions started out, say about 1650, with the higher population and greater industrial employment in the south. The subsequent divergence led to lower incomes in the southern countryside and more emigration, though the outflow was too small to raise average incomes to northern levels. Southern farmers pioneered technical changes in husbandry in the seventeenth and eighteenth centuries but were to face severe competition from New World cereals during the arable depression from the 1870s to 1939, which was interrupted only in 1914-1922. The story of regional differentiation is not unlike the history of nineteenth and twentieth century Italy. Regional inversion is however largely omitted from textbooks about England and the initially greater prosperity and industrialism of the south tends to come as a surprise to those accustomed to the certainties of the northern industrial revolution.

The Highland Zone – the north, or more strictly north and west – had high relief, old and hard rocks, soils that were often thin, and a cool, wet climate. Grain grown there was too dear to compete with the south in third markets. The south had *locational* advantages: it was closer to the main pre-industrial markets. Much the biggest of these was the international trading port of London, as well as the Netherlands, to which malting barley could be shipped from south-eastern ports. In addition there were districts containing numbers of out-workers in domestic industry, who worked in their own homes and had to buy the grain they consumed. The south also had the *site* advantages of lower, gentler topography, better soils and a dryer, warmer climate, which made for lower costs of cereal production and somewhat lower transport and communication costs, whether by canalized river, canals or turnpike roads.

Where land was suitable for grain which could be profitably transported to London or to markets overseas, landowners were keen to establish the large farms which they thought most efficient for growing cereals. They resisted copyhold tenure and devised methods to undermine it. Hence in these areas the land was increasingly consolidated into large farms. Small farmers began to disappear but the villages were preserved. The agricultural population came to consist of a few working farmers, who mostly did not own their land, and their skilled workers, plus a larger number of poor villagers who supplied the labour to work in the fields and harvest the crops in summer. Many worked at manufacturing at home in the winter, for example weaving.[7] In the south and east some districts were pastoral, with dairying and sheep farming. In those areas, woollen manufacturing and other industries were still expanding in the seventeenth century.

Initially, southerners were startled by the wildness of society in the 'dark corners of the land' of the far north and west, so different from Dutch-like East Anglia.[8] But that was in the far corners and gives no hint of the growth potential becoming evident in much of south Lancashire and Cheshire. Some of the impetus stemmed from the independent-mindedness of a society of small farmers. The ecological basis lay in the fact that the western side of England from Cumbria to Devon was pastoral, although the south-west did retain a substantial arable area. In most pastoral areas there seemed little incentive to make larger farms and a three-life leasehold system became established. This approximately divided the income from the land between landlord and tenant.[9] The arrangement created a society in the north-west where about two-thirds of families had some capital. This surprising finding emerges from an analysis of the rare 1660 Poll Tax returns for the Northwich Hundred in Cheshire and the Blackburn Hundred in Lancashire. Combining the Poll Tax figures with those of the Hearth Tax of 1664 allows a large sample of 7,181 families to be surveyed.[10]

London was the largest market and the centre to which English manufactures were sent for redistribution within the country, partly because it was the hub of coastal shipping as well as of the road system. London was also the greatest port. Goods for export were sent there and imported goods were distributed to the rest of the country. But this dominance had other effects. London's ballooning population and high cost of living, combined with crowded, unhealthy conditions for the poor, led to high mortality.

---

[7] Spufford, 1974, pp 67 – 71.
[8] Phillips, 1999, pp.43 & 375.
[9] Foster, 2004, p 58.
[10] Foster, 2004, pp 144 - 151; Foster, see below, Part II, p 73.

Wages had to be raised substantially to attract workers. By 1700 wages in London were two to three times higher than in the north and west of the country and this effect lasted until about 50 miles from the centre.[11] It influenced the location of manufacturing - for example only the final stages of clothing manufacture could be carried out profitably in London. A tailor there could cut and sew a gentleman's suit but the cloth, the linings, the buttons and the thread were made more than 50 miles away.

Throughout the seventeenth and eighteenth centuries manufacturing in London moved up the value chain, replacing certain products with higher-value finished goods.[12] During the seventeenth and eighteenth centuries fustians, framework knitting, silk- and handkerchief-making, and shoe-making were all successively relinquished to the provinces. The high-value goods that replaced them included coaches and mathematical instruments. London had long been the grand centre of luxury consumption and it was joined in the eighteenth century by spa resorts and racing towns, which drained still more purchasing power away from the market towns. Craftsmen in the smaller places were usually the sufferers.

The forces pushing manufacturing out into the rest of the country did however create opportunities for regional specialization. A good example is the framework knitting industry which produced hosiery. Machines for this work had been invented in the Nottingham area in Elizabeth's reign. The work left London and for more than three centuries became concentrated around Nottingham, Derby and Leicester, despite the fact that the original product – knitted silk stockings – was sold almost exclusively to the very rich in London. This specialization allowed an intensive division of labour to develop so that by 1739 frame-smiths, setters-up, sinker makers, stocking needle makers, joiners and turners were as numerous as the stockingers who operated the machines.[13]

---

[11] Gilboy, 1934, pp 10 - 12, 95, 107, 180 - 3.
[12] Jones, 2010, p 242; Rollison, 2011, p 265.
[13] Chambers, 1932, p 95.

Industry and trade had expanded in the second half of the sixteenth century.   Woollen industries were on the rise throughout the Lowland Zone (east, south and west) until the first decade of the next century, but in 1614 royal interference – in particular the Cockayne project – dealt a severe blow to woollen cloth exports in particular. This was soon followed by Charles I's personal rule. Between 1620 and 1641 about 80,000 people, 2 per cent of the population, left England, one quarter of them going to New England. They were mostly well-off people and many were in trade or were skilled craftsmen from the textile areas in the eastern counties or the West of England. A large proportion consisted of disgruntled Puritans from within a fifty-mile radius of Groton, Suffolk, which lies within the Lowland Zone or 'south'.[14] Their decision probably stemmed from uncertainty as to whether their property, religion and way of life would be secure under the King.[15]

The Civil War and Commonwealth period was a watershed. Following Charles I's execution, vigorous business activity was quickly resumed and from then on increased in volume and became more or less continuous. Because a majority of the old gentry had supported the King their influence in the countryside was diminished. In Cheshire, for example, the old manorial rule that tenants could not let their land to 'strangers' fell into disuse and three-life leaseholders were able to rent out their land, leave off farming and invest their capital and energy in other businesses.

Standard histories emphasize political contention yet the economy shrugged off much of it. Despite the wrangling, apprehensions and genuine threats that persisted as late as 1745, investment must have seemed fairly secure right from 1650. The Cromwellian elite certainly thought so and was emboldened to erect a surprising number of country houses during the 1650s (with 'ostentatious humility of design' but fine buildings nevertheless).[16] Charles II's settlement confirmed their luck. The military officers who had

---

[14] Phillips, 1999, pp 18 & 22.
[15] Fischer, 1989, pp 28 - 36.
[16] Mowl & Earnshaw, 1995.

bought land during the Commonwealth may have lost most of it, except in Ireland, but merchant families were typically able to hold what they had acquired. Investment rose on all fronts after the Restoration and especially after the 'elite settlement' following the Glorious Revolution of 1688. Adam Smith felt able to call the years between 1660 and 1760, 'the happiest and most fortunate period of them all.'[17]

The contrast with the time of the Civil Wars was stark. By the end of the wars there had been several massacres, more than 150 towns and 50 villages had been damaged or burned down, 200 country houses had been ruined and over 50,000 people made homeless.[18] Enormous uncertainty clouded investment decisions. It may not be surprising therefore that only two Acts for river improvement were passed during the Civil War and the Commonwealth period. This activity required big expenditures with long gestation periods and relied on coordinated agreement among many landowners, which was more awkward than, say, building stand-alone mansions or even repairing damage to dwellings in the towns, as happened in the 1650s. During the sixteenth century there had been eight Acts for river improvement and after 1660 activity was virtually continuous, with particular bursts in 1662-1665, 1697-1700 and 1719-1721. This suggests that the 1640s and to some extent the 1650s formed little more than a lull during the early phases of a long upward trend.[19]

J. R. Green quoted the post-Restoration bishop of Salisbury, Burnet, as acknowledging the economic achievement of the Commonwealth: 'We always reckon those eight years of the usurpation a time of great peace and prosperity.'[20] Close-up they do not look serene years, politically-speaking, but they do exhibit considerable pent-up demand, as does the rebuilding of towns in the 1650s and 1660s. A favourable view of the Commonwealth period pushes back the onset of Adam Smith's happy and fortunate

---

[17] Smith, 1776 Book 2, Ch 3, p 35.
[18] Coster, 1999, pp 91 - 92; Porter, 1994.
[19] Willan, 1936, pp 28 - 30.
[20] Green, 1898, p 589.

period. The closer we look, the more the period 1614 to 1650 appears as a tragic interruption to an expansion that had been taking place since at least Elizabeth's reign. After Charles I was executed, and of course after the Restoration, investment in infrastructure resumed, with each generation able to hand the next a superior endowment. A key point is that this activity was in train even before the Glorious Revolution of 1688.

3 The concentration of industry in the north-west

In the north-west manufacturing activity resumed too. Examination of four of the important activities developed there between 1500 and 1780 shows that their growth was the result of the vigorous entrepreneurship and innovative skills of local families who had started to have a little capital at their command in the late sixteenth century. The industries sold to quite distant markets and obtained some of their raw materials from a distance, even from overseas. West Country clay went to the Potteries by sailing ship to Runcorn until the Second World War, an observation that encapsulates much of what was taking place: a northern industry expanding while the south was reduced to supplying some of its raw materials. Existing industries in the south began to shrink. Deindustrialization was a prolonged affair and the detailed timing varied from trade to trade and place to place. But between c.1650 and c.1850, as we shall see, southern deindustrialization was plain, despite occasional recoveries, some exceptions and a handful of counter-movements.

In the north-west, however, all was growth. First among four of the most important activities, the industry that became known in the 1780 to 1800 period as 'engineering' began early alongside the rich coal mines of the Wigan area. By the 1550s a metal-using industry had been producing brass and pewter pots and pans for the kitchens of the better off; by 1590 bronze bells were being cast.[21] Iron was also being cut into nails and blacksmiths were widespread. The metals had to be imported into the Mersey, probably to Warrington. In the 1590s the watch and clock business

---

[21] Latham, 2009, pp 260 - 3; Cheshire & Lancs Record Office.; many local inventories from 1550.

began near Liverpool, no doubt using metals from the same sources. By 1599 Thomas Dallam, from the Warrington area, travelled to Constantinople with a clockwork organ which he had made, as a present from Queen Elizabeth to the Sultan Mehmet III.[22] By the 1680s many special tools had been developed, including one that cut the teeth of watch and clock wheels more accurately than could be done by hand. Elaborate watches were certainly crafted in London but from that period on it is likely that most of the watches and clocks sold in England included parts, if not whole movements, made in the north-west.[23]

The brass industry became more competitive in 1719, when Thomas Patten built a copper-smelting works in Warrington to act as a local supplier of metal for the casting and rolling industry.[24] The watch, clock and tool-making industries were carried on by hundreds, perhaps thousands, of craftsmen-entrepreneurs typically living on their own properties within 20 miles of Prescot, South Lancashire. Most concentrated on producing only one or two components or tools or assemblies and developed highly specialized equipment and skills.[25] About 500 different tools are illustrated in John Wyke's catalogues of the 1750s.[26]

The second industry was cheese-making. From 1500 until the mid-seventeenth century most of the cheese consumed in London had come from Suffolk. In the late 1640s cattle disease in Suffolk opened the way for a 20-ton cargo of Cheshire cheese to be sent to the capital in 1650. Its rich full milk taste won it a market and by 1687 a total of about 1,800 tons per year was going south. By 1729 Cheshire was supplying nearly 60 per cent of London's cheese and less than 10 per cent came from Suffolk.[27] Before the 1780s cheese

---

[22] Dalham, 1893.

[23] Bailey & Barker, 1969, pp 7 - 8; Musson & Robinson, 1969, pp 427 - 458.

[24] Foster, 2004, pp 211 - 12.

[25] Ashton, 1939 , pp 1 - 8; Foster, 2004, pp 304 - 5.

[26] John Wyke, Catalogue (1758 - 1782), printed for Winterthur Museum by University Press of Virginia, Charlottesville, 1978.

[27] Foster, 1998, pp 6 - 7, 22 & 91.

was the principal farm product of the whole of the Dee and Mersey basins.[28]

Cheshire farms were enlarged from an average of 25 to 30 acres to between 65 to 100 acres, which was the most efficient size for producing the large cheeses that Londoners liked. There was a big advance in productivity. The number of acres needed to support one dairy cow was reduced from about 10 in the 1700s to about 6.5 by the 1760s and the annual quantity of cheese produced per cow rose from 2 cwt. in 1717-1719 to 2.5-3 cwt. by the end of the century.[29] Improvements in transport were also significant. North-western farms provided the grassland for cart-horses as well as cows, and it was northern horses that were normally used for road transport to London. Various factors allowed an increase in the weight one cart could draw. In 1672 carts carried only 10-12 cwt. of coal the twenty miles from Staffordshire to Northwich. In 1761 the carts bringing coal sixteen miles from Haydock to Arley carried one ton each. These gains were presumably due to innovations in the design and manufacture of the cart, the harness and the road.[30]

The third industry was the production of salt. From the Conquest onwards the large profits made from producing salt in the Cheshire 'wich' towns (the largest being Nantwich) were divided between the King and the local gentry. From the 1590s onwards sources of salt outside the wiches began to be exploited. By 1680 major works around Northwich, using the latest technology, were exporting 1,000 tons per year. In 1694 a revenue-raising tax scheme suggested by the manufacturers, which taxed all salt but kept out foreign supplies, helped production soar to over 10,000 tons per year. [31] In the 1730s and again in the 1750s two local businessmen engaged in the salt industry made large investments in waterways – the Weaver Navigation (1730-1732) and the Sankey Navigation (1755-1758). These enabled Cheshire salt to become

[28] Foster, 1998, pp 8 - 9 & 24.
[29] Foster, 1998, pp 12 - 16, & 25 - 6.
[30] Cheshire Record Office, DCH/J/112, Leftwich Eyes accounts 1672; Estate invoices Oct 1761, see www.arleyhallarchives.co.uk.
[31] Collins, 1682.

the cheapest in the world.[32]   Cheese and salt were the cargoes that transformed Liverpool from a small fishing port with only 1,000 inhabitants in 1660.   But it was the entrepreneurial foresight of its merchants, who built a Wet Dock there between 1709 and 1720, that enabled the town to capture the American trade and become a city of 34,000 people by 1770.[33]   Continual innovations turned the Cheshire salt industry from the antique relic of 1590 into a most competitive business by 1760.   Similar processes of innovation were repeated in all the other industries.

The fourth industry was cotton manufacture.   Linen had always been produced in the area from the flax or hemp grown on every farm.   In the sixteenth century it was taken to market by strings of horses which went south to visit any community that did not produce its own linen.[34]   When raw cotton first arrived in London in bulk from the Levant around 1600, Lancashire weavers seized the opportunity to start making jeans and denims, known as fustians, using their linen for the warp and cotton for the weft.[35]

Every year after 1651 ships returning to the Mersey to collect cheese brought cargoes from London that transformed industry in the north-west, for instance dye-stuffs from all over the world became available to the textile industries.[36]   Meanwhile agriculture was enabled to specialize in a way that encouraged the manufacturing of cotton.   Grain crops, particularly barley, do not grow well in the area.   It had not been possible to import them because there were no balancing exports.   Cheese filled the gap: from the 1650s Cheshire could concentrate its agriculture on what suited it best – grassland dairy farming.   Being able to import grain supported the population engaged in the cotton industry, which had arrived in the Bolton-Blackburn area about 1600.   Before 1500 these moorland valleys had been very thinly populated because of the difficulty of growing grain.   Once it became possible to import

---

[32] Foster, 2004, pp 186 - 98 & 224 - 7.
[33] Power, 2000, pp 51 - 71.
[34] Withersby, 1998.
[35] Foster, see below, Part II, p 66-79.
[36] The National Archives E 190 Port Books.

this, new settlers moved into the hill country to supply the labour for spinning the imported cotton and weaving the finished fustians.[37]

The cotton manufacturing industry was buffeted by extraordinary events. From about 1670 the market was flooded with great quantities of cheap coloured cotton fabrics from India. These caused so much disruption to textile markets that large duties were imposed and finally in 1721 the wearing of any dyed or printed cotton except traditional fustians was prohibited. But in 1736 manufacturers secured a new Act permitting them to make dyed and printed cloths with a linen warp and cotton weft. This set the industry off on a remarkable innovative phase. By the 1750s it had the best skills in Europe and John Holker was selling these skills to the French.[38] Customers loved the new dyed and printed cloths and the market for cotton expanded two and a half times in twenty-five years. By the late 1760s there was a really serious shortage of spinners.[39] Three craftsmen – Hargreaves, Crompton and Highs - made prototype machines and the long-established Lancashire engineering industry developed them into spinning machinery. (Highs designed the model which Arkwright patented, as described at the trial of his patents in 1785).[40] Their efforts were so successful that 900 mills were at work by 1797 and a new world of manufacturing machinery had been created.[41]

Only with hindsight can these developments be made to seem a 'natural' or continuous evolution, without sudden jumps on both the demand and supply sides. Nevertheless a key element was the prior emergence of the highly skilled workers in the south Lancashire watch and clock industries. They solved horological problems empirically, though little is known in detail of their achievements, as much as anything because they were individual craftsmen working in their own small premises rather than in large

---

[37] Foster, see below, Part II, pp 75-6.
[38] Montgomery, 1984, p 395 & Colour Plates D22-D33 of 36 samples.
[39] Foster, see below, Part II, pp 84-6.
[40] Fitton, 1989, pp 14 - 17, & 128 - 9.
[41] The National Archive, 30/8/187, H. Watts to William Pitt.

firms which, when successful, would see to their own publicity. What is known, and is of the first importance, is that some of them were hired to solve the problems of early cotton machinery.

4   Why did these developments, or their equivalents, not happen elsewhere?

Here we consider the four types of industry that have already been mentioned, this time with reference to alternative locations. But we defer for the moment the question of what was happening to the economy of southern England.

Metalwork: Many places had coal and the Black Country also had its own iron ore and numbers of similar metal-workers. However a watch, clock and tool industry did not develop there. Since so little fuel was required for these industries they might have expected to settle on the coast somewhere much nearer to the principal market in London. Perhaps the north-western location was due to the large number of owner-occupied properties in the Prescot area. Young men were apprenticed to clock and tool makers, afterwards building workshops next to their houses and setting up their own businesses making one or two types of tool, component, or assembly. Groups of small properties where this could have been done were rare in the south.[42]

Cheese: Cheshire did not have a monopoly of making cheese, which was also made on many farms in Gloucestershire, Somerset and Wiltshire. In the eighteenth century cheese was shipped to London down the Thames from a warehouse at Buscot near Lechlade. This was close to the head of navigation and collected cheese brought to it from further west in Gloucestershire, as well as from the Upper Thames district and the Vale of White Horse (close to Buscot), into which the technique of making 'Double Gloucester' spread. Yet even in 1729 this area supplied less than one quarter of London's cheese.[43] Cheddar, whose brand came to dominate the London market in the nineteenth century, is only

---

[42] Foster, 1992, pp 11 - 13 & 55 - 78; Lawton, 1979, Lancs Record Office, Blackburn Hundred Poll Tax 1660 & Hearth Tax 1664, typed copies.
[43] Foster, 1998, pp 22 & 24.

eleven or twelve miles from the sea at Weston-super-Mare. Nevertheless, Cheddar did not oust Cheshire from the London market until north-western farmers turned their attention to feeding the huge industrial populations emerging in the north.

Salt: Ancient brine springs, very similar to those in Cheshire, were also worked at Droitwich, Worcestershire. This was only about five miles from the river Severn. Had a canal been built in the 1690s, the Severn route could have provided both coal and access to the sea, which would have made Droitwich salt much cheaper than that of Northwich. Droitwich men managed to increase their share of the national market from 5 per cent in 1694 to 20 per cent in 1730, after which their share declined. They were apparently unable to navigate the maze of legal rights and did not build a canal until the 1770s, by which time it was too late.[44] In the north-west, businessmen and the old gentry worked together successfully to promote industry and the local gentry MPs helped get Canal Acts through Parliament.[45] And just as Droitwich failed to make a fist of salt production compared with the north-west, so the brine salt industry at Lymington on the Hampshire coast faded into the abandoned salterns that are mere archaeological traces today.

Cotton: Once raw cotton started arriving in London about 1600, in bulk directly from the Levant, cotton cloth could have been manufactured in many places. Worcestershire, Somerset and Dorset all had suitable linen industries and Pontefract in Yorkshire was the centre of a large linen area only 20 miles from navigable water on the River Ouse. Yet cotton was transported 200 miles overland from London to Manchester. Why? One plausible reason for the extraordinary vigour of the north-west seems to lie in the peculiar character of its society. As we have seen, this was highly relevant to the structure of enterprise, and to its regional vigour. From 1550 this was a society with a large number of small farming families each with a little capital; it continued to be organized like this, with many thousands of small cheese-producing farms. The industries that grew up were likewise numerous and small-scale.

---

[44] British Library Add Mss 36914.
[45] Foster, 2004, pp 194, 198 & 320.

Much of the metal-working was carried out by independent businesses and so was cotton production: Manchester had over 500 textile businesses by 1773.[46] Unit costs were doubtless kept down by the sheer volume of transactions and the density of the supporting trades that clustered around.

The wide distribution of wealth fostered a spirit of equality and religious participation unfriendly to the hierarchical framework of the Anglican Church. The church was weaker in the north because of the very large parishes and their low populations, together (depending on the precise district) with their low cereal productivity. Before and during the Civil War there were numerous Puritan ministers in the business districts who became Dissenters in 1662. Their congregations stayed loyal to them and after 1689 many chapels were built, where the congregation itself appointed the minister. Quakers and Unitarians were prominent among the leaders of the business community. The atmosphere even influenced local Anglicans, who in Warrington (in a type of imitation not unknown among competing sects at many periods) also built their own chapel and appointed the minister.

The law in Cheshire and Lancashire was administered from the Palatinate courts in Chester and Preston and offered little scope to London lawyers. Government of the counties was in the hands of old gentry JPs, who normally lived in the area and rarely went to London. There were few openings in the Church or the Law and also few in Government. The local gentry had poor connections with the court, the Ministry and the armed services. This meant that many of the job opportunities for educated people which existed in the London area were not available in the north-west. Business became the principal occupation. Dissenting congregations, composed of business people, celebrated the value of lives well spent in commerce and stressed the importance of moral behaviour – honesty, integrity, equal treatment for all, men and women - in principle giving everyone an opportunity to do well in life. Nothing comparable characterized the highly unequal, squire- and parson- (or 'squarson') dominated south.

---

[46] Wadsworth & Mann, 1931, pp 254 - 260.

During the seventeenth and eighteenth centuries business values permeated north-western society, irrespective of religious affiliation. Families stayed in the same businesses, sons and grandsons succeeding to capital investments made decades earlier. People cared about their businesses and, if they had no sons, found a nephew or cousin or even trained up a young stranger to carry it on. An example was the Crosfield family, who were brought from Kendal to Warrington in 1777 and stayed to run the businesses there until the 1920s. Joseph Crosfield & Sons Ltd, now part of Unilever, is still the biggest firm in the town. When families in the north-west became very rich they did not buy estates in the country and pose as old gentry; they built themselves big houses in the towns close to their factories, like the Pattens in Warrington and several families in Manchester.[47] Some Quakers were even less self-indulgent; there was only a modest Crosfield house in a nearby village. These attitudes and practices created a business culture in north-western England (and the northern colonies of America) which was one of the keys to the enterprise in these areas before 1780.

5 Why not a southern location?

Subsequently the industrial revolution was so successful that leading families in the north-west became extremely rich – far surpassing the wealth of most others in business before 1780. With their wealth they eventually started to mingle more with rich people in the south and adopt their lifestyle: they became gentry. This starts to indicate one reason why industry was so much less successful in the south, a region that not only failed to capitalize on the growth of a national market for manufactures, but conspicuously under-invested in its people, and actually de-industrialized during the eighteenth and nineteenth centuries. Plant in the south was tiny (though industrial works everywhere were small before the age of powered factories) but was widespread and included the full range of industries existing at the period. They slowly but surely died back, perhaps taking 20 per cent to 30 per

---

[47] Foster, 2004, pp 262 - 3, Plates 22, 29, 33-4, detailed maps of Warrington & notes 40-43.

cent of small southern towns with them; there was a marked shake-out of smaller centres, which lost their status and much of their function. [48] By the late eighteenth century the larger towns seem to have housed the more competitive businesses.

It is important to recognize that in 1650 the south had been the richer as well as the more populous and industrial of the two main regions. Eight of the ten largest provincial cities were located there, whereas by 1860 eight of the top ten were in the north. Given the limitations of transport and communications it is hardly surprising that in the seventeenth century the south largely supplied its own industrial products. Motive power was limited to human and animal energy, with help from occasional mill sites on the sluggish streams of the lowlands. But during the two hundred years after 1650, industry retreated in the south. Notice 'in' the south rather than 'from' the south since, although there was a little direct migration of firms to the north, much of what happened was an outcome of the competition-induced concentration of production in larger and larger towns within the south. Manufacturing in smaller places withered away and sometimes the places themselves stood still. Eventually enterprises in the bigger southern towns shrank too, and the country as a whole became largely supplied by even bigger works and powered factories in the north.

The outcome was not simply the result of superior northern competition and most definitely not an outcome of the eventual adoption of steam engines by manufacturers. The relevant competitive process had long been under way through subtle developments that are largely 'under the radar', to use the cant expression, of modern economic historians. To repeat, a large part of the change was the result of a competition among southern producers which was successively won by the larger among them, who seem to have reaped economies of scale. The sources of their advantage are admittedly hard to pin down. The tiny enterprises and vanished firms of the time left few primary sources, while companies that fail to survive rarely commission self-vaunting business histories like those written about the industrial colossi of

---

[48] Borsay (ed.), 1990, pp 5 - 6.

the twentieth century. Plenty of examples of outright invention in the south may nevertheless be found - the defect was limited innovation, which is to say that typically they were not put into the production process. Fewer mentions survive of the incremental improvements in business organization and routines, nevertheless a 'meta-analysis' of both contemporary and modern published works does uncover some of them. One was the halving of the time it took to prepare hides for tanning, developed in a tannery at Wantage, Berkshire, right at the start of the nineteenth century.[49] This is not a happy example since the tannery soon became spectacularly bankrupt but in general the competitive advantage of the larger southern enterprises does appear to have been partly the accumulation of such small and largely unsung improvements in technique and organization.

What, then, was it that dwindled away? Glass-making in the Weald went early in the seventeenth century, though partly because one entrepreneur secured a monopoly patent and preferred to set up business in Newcastle. The fact that his use of coal probably did later reduce costs does not show that he was more efficient to start with and for a long time the mass production of glass suffered in favour of fancy ware. Iron-making also quit the Weald but did not wholly leave the south: the pivotal invention of the industrial revolution period was Henry Cort's discovery of how to puddle iron at Gosport, Hampshire, at the end of the eighteenth century. Tanning also shrank into larger and larger tan-yards in Northamptonshire and London. If tanning no longer sounds a major industry, consider the range of leather goods needed by a horse-drawn economy and the fact that making leather was still the fourth largest industry by value in 1851.

The list goes on: stocking knitting concentrated tightly in Nottinghamshire and Leicestershire, quitting London and elsewhere, leaving only an isolated rump in Tewkesbury, Gloucestershire. Ship-building, once the pride of tiny south coast 'hards', faded away. Pin-making, for which Gloucester was the national centre into the nineteenth century, finally went. Far and

---

[49] Hammond, 1974, pp 54 - 55.

away the biggest complex of industries, textiles, died a lingering death. They shifted down to cheaper and poorer quality goods like 'shalloons', although the great mills of the Stroud valley, at one time the largest units of the type in the country, did survive until they closed in a rush about 1830, despite having adopted the steam engine. The water-powered mills and other plant manufacturing cotton goods (fustian) also withered on the southern vine.

Consider, too, what may seem a minor trade, bell-founding. Here, the big battalions won once more, when the Whitechapel foundry, oldest in the country, bought up a number of provincial bell-founders and did away with their competition by simply closing them down. This trade enables us to establish the point that enterprise in making things was not absolutely absent from the south. Among southern bell-founders, Benjamin Franklin's uncle, Thomas, was a partner in the Bagley family firm that cast 441 bells at Chacombe, east of Banbury. Benjamin caught the temper of his kin when he wrote of his own son, 'I don't want him to be what is commonly called a gentleman... I want to put him to some business by which he may, with care and industry, get a temperate and reasonable living.'[50] What could be more like the business culture of the north-west? But the gentry culture prevailed in the south and Benjamin Franklin's father emigrated to New England.

No one explanation by itself will account for all these examples; not direct northern competition, not coal and not the steam engine. The Victorians nevertheless thought that coal fully explained the dazzling northern growth of their day and hence accounted for industrial decline elsewhere, but this interpretation is at least partly anachronistic. The naturalist, William Buckland, even claimed that the great mineral wealth of Britain showed the Almighty's intention that it should become the richest and most powerful nation. But his was the fallacy of thinking history leads up to the circumstances of one's own day and then comes to a halt. The remarks here are not meant to diminish the burst of (almost wholly) nineteenth-century productivity growth which the classic industrial revolution was to see embodied in powered machinery and the

---

[50] www.ectonvillage.co.uk/bfranklin.html; Bliss, 2003, pp 11-22.

factory system. Their purpose is to put industrial growth in the north and industrial decay in the south into perspective and show that they were prolonged affairs resulting from gradually growing competition in the economy as a whole. The manufacturing use of coal intruded into, piggy-backed on, and of course mightily magnified a process of market competition already long under way.

Underlying this were two factors: the rise of a business culture in the north and the stultifying of such a culture (or its redirection to the agricultural sector) in the south; and the emergence of larger and larger market areas, knitting eventually into one national market, of which the physical basis was improved transport and communications: canalized rivers, canals and turnpike roads. Railways came later. The eventual speeding up of change notwithstanding, our model does not rely on magic bullets – it rests on multiple interacting developments akin to modern conceptions of the subtle way in which economic development really works.[51] Thus no one explanation of the conventional single-factor type will account for the industrial revolution or the die-back of southern industry. Many suggestions that have been put forward to account for deindustrialization tend to reflect only secondary responses to a loss of competitiveness.[52] The deeper causes were twofold: first, the culture of the gentry that pervaded the south and hampered industry, and secondly the shift in comparative advantage which led to the region becoming more purely agricultural.

A significant element was indeed the strong influence of the gentry in the wide hinterland of London.[53] Money earned, or at any rate acquired, in the metropolis was spent on buying and remodelling landed estates in the Home Counties. Bristol money, including profits from the slave trade, performed a similar function inland of that city. London was, however, the fount of most gain because to commercial wealth it added the proceeds of government office, the law and innumerable court sinecures. This is not to say that every fortune was ruralized but the tendency was marked. Country

---

[51] Banerjee & Duflo, 2011; Radelet, 2010.
[52] Jones, 2010, chs. 4 & 5.
[53] Jones, 2012.

houses were built and rebuilt, and equipped with fashionable furniture, besides antiquities and art work often brought back from the Grand Tour. Between 1760 and 1820 the number of parks in the Home Counties doubled and while parkland was often mown or grazed, it cannot be held that this was its optimal agricultural use. Some of the grazing beasts were merely ornamental, like herds of fallow deer. Capability Brown alone constructed 150 ornamental lakes. Even the Puritan elite had hastened to build themselves grand parkland houses while, in the eighteenth century, part of Berkshire was dubbed 'the Berkshire Hindoostan' because of the number of nabobs who repatriated their loot to build country houses there. The attractions of owning an estate were high; it was the thing to do, offering useful contacts, access to financially advantageous marriage partners, political opportunities, and country amenities, among them participation in the rage for hunting, shooting and angling.

In practice anyone with sufficient capital could enter landed society, providing they were willing to ape prevalent manners and consumption habits. They could bring up their sons as country gentlemen and hope to see their daughters marry old money. The point was that they or their offspring were losing the impetus for making money in any active sense and were becoming rentiers, that is to say joining Veblen's leisure class. A proportion of them did take an interest in the management of their estates, especially when agriculture became fashionable under George III, and some became farming enthusiasts. Royal approval validated their interest, as it were, though it is likely monarch and subject were jointly affected by expanding opportunities to experiment during the late eighteenth century. An unknown number brought back ideas and even seeds they had acquired when mixing with their fellows during the London season. An example was Edward Wallwyn of Much Marcle, Herefordshire, who in 1795 wrote to his agent enclosing some turnip seed, 'a Single Pound of a New Sort, called *The Sweedish Turnip'*, which he wished to see tried out on his land and that of some neighbours. 'I must have a fair Trial made of this single Pound… Desire Mr Crump', Wallwyn wrote, ' to put out a

Bit of Ground… & sow some of the Seed.'[54] Within ten years swedes were being grown fairly widely in Herefordshire and their hardiness improved the winter food supplies of livestock.

6 Landed investment

Agricultural management in the estate system was nevertheless ambivalent. Men like Wallwyn may have encouraged innovation but against that innumerable landowners or their agents protected the non-agricultural values of landscaping and blood sports in ways that restricted productive opportunities.[55] Southern agriculture had been developing at the hands of practical farmers long before the time of George III and his landowning cronies. Day-to-day farming remained the province of bailiffs and tenants. The direct commercial risks were passed down from landowners to their tenant farmers.

Investments in land went into building vast stables and kennels, laying out parks, and ornamenting estates with lakes and copses. The last point indicates where the thrust was: creating a gracious landscape which was simultaneously the setting for blood sports. This meant planting woods and hedges to facilitate hunting and shooting. It involved conflict with any aim of maximizing output from the estates: tenants were often required to adopt rotations consistent with the demands of game-keeping rather than husbandry, while well-grown young trees were removed from the woods to use in purely ornamental groves.[56] The costs did not matter acutely to most landowners, since farming was seldom their leading motive for possessing an estate. Estates were thus the joint products of stylized rural consumption and agricultural endeavour. On the estates and in the parks capital was used less productively than it might have been, let alone what it might have earned in industry. This is indicated by the appellation of Gentlemen Clothiers for the woollen manufacturers who bought rural properties near their mills in Gloucestershire and is consistent with the impression that estates commonly produced an annual return of

---

[54] Jones, 1974, p 51.
[55] Jones, 2009, pp 51 - 56.
[56] Grayson & Jones, 1955, p 22.

only about 2 per cent. Admittedly the tendency for successful industrialists to buy estates was not confined to the south but it was most conspicuous within reach of London.

Eventually, in Victorian times, many a successful entrepreneur from the industrial north sought to distance himself and his family, physically and socially, from the place of his profitable striving. London lawyers, courtiers, office-holders and merchants had long done the same, as had some of the most prosperous among the first generation of factory owners: very early in the nineteenth century the Arkwrights, cotton spinners, bought five estates widely dispersed across England. The movement of northern money, especially from Lancashire, to estates in the south, notably to Gloucestershire, was so marked in Victorian times as to make us suspect a chain reaction or snowball effect. These incomers were willing and able, sometimes rashly so, to make a splash in the countryside – to buy acceptance – by spending heavily on estate buildings, farm houses and landscape adornments. It reinforced the partial conversion of whole districts into landscapes of consumption.

The attractions of county society were immensely powerful. There was of course a London season but during the remainder of the year rural residence was not scorned. Estates provided plenty of displacement activities for the rich: they sat on the bench, dined and danced together in their houses or the assembly rooms of county towns, and engaged in rural sports. Few can be accused of complete idleness; what they can be accused of is expending their talents on trivial activities and making them seem the ultimate purposes in life. They formed a leisure class that retained only peripheral connections with anything productive, other than farming, and was devoted to its own reproduction: read the southern author, Jane Austen. Fashion and snobbery drew the ambitious to embrace a way of life consistent with aristocratic rurality.

If the businessman himself was not very interested, his wife and children were likely to press for gentility rather than endeavour. Country towns depended heavily on the patronage of the landed class and serviced their wants as well as the needs of agriculture. Feasts, dining on a fallow buck provided by a local magnate, helped to bind town to country. Yet as merchants and industrialists removed themselves from town to countryside they made way for new men to push upwards and secure commercial and industrial fortunes for themselves. County society, full of landed families both old and parvenu, was willing to embrace the owners of new money but was hostile to industry on the doorstep. The question remains, why did estates come on the market if the lifestyle and maybe the agricultural prospects were so attractive? Little or no systematic work seems to have been done on outgoing owners. The supply of estates was tight and prices were forced up, but properties did come onto the market when family lines died out or failed to produce suitable heirs. Some owners wished to concentrate on estates they owned elsewhere and others were too deeply in debt not to sell. The capital that went out of the sector was presumably dispersed among urban creditors. No matter: public office and the associated corrupt takings, and increasingly the profits of industry, eagerly replaced any outflow.

Despite the element of consumption on landed estates, the south was nevertheless a developing agricultural region. Relative to the north, a better natural endowment made it more conducive to arable farming. It was significant that the south was well placed to supply the market for foodstuffs in the capital. Grain was also supplied to the dense rural populations engaged in manufacturing in various parts of the countryside, especially domestic spinning and weaving, but it was the London market that came to dominate. As noted, investment in canalized rivers, canals, better roads and turnpikes was directed at supplying it.

Farming, in which the south came to specialize, was an immensely varied and complicated activity involving thousands of small or at most medium-sized businesses. Generations of dispute about when agriculture experienced a 'revolution', and how this may have affected industrialization, have almost certainly been misplaced. The process was instead one of knowledge accumulating on a slowly mounting curve. Direct interventions such as that by landowners like Wallwyn in Herefordshire apart, change was as much as anything via 'stimulus diffusion', that is, imitating methods that had been watched in neighbours' fields or simply heard described. Formal experiment and agricultural extension services scarcely existed. Encouragement via non-pecuniary rewards - prizes at shows - started to appear in the second half of the eighteenth century but were prone to the 'prize marrow fallacy' which exalted technical achievement (the largest marrow) over proven profitability. It is hardly to be expected that the customizing of innumerable husbandry practices on myriad farm units distributed across different geological strata, soil types and topographical formations could be anything other than gradual.

That is what took place, however, and it took place disproportionately across the south, articulated around William Cobbett's expanding 'great wen' of the London market. The nutrient cycle in London is informative. The city needed to be fed and also needed to feed what was in total a vast herd of horses. One aspect of the cycle was as follows: the horse population was supplied with hay and straw brought, say, up the Thames from Essex by sailing barge. Dung from the horses later went by boat or wagon to the market gardens of Middlesex, from which the produce went to Smithfield and other markets in order to feed the Londoners themselves.[57]

This touches on the central issue for agriculture: how can the fertility taken out of the soil in the form of crops and livestock be replenished? To simplify, from the seventeenth century soil fertility in country farming districts was upgraded using the dung of the sheepfold. Sheep were fed less and less on down-land grass and more and more on new fodder crops, many of which had begun productive life as market garden vegetables. These crops, clover, turnips, the swedes about which Wallwyn wrote, and so forth, were inserted by trial and error into a kaleidoscopic array of rotations, some courses of which were the cereals required for bread and beer, i.e. wheat and barley. Organizational changes also took place that seem to have raised productivity but we may note how the chief of these, enclosure, has received excessive billing among the

---

[57] Thick, 1998, pp 101 - 102.

list of developments, possibly because it generated so many documents and has excited controversy among historians for well over one hundred years. Enclosure was a somewhat ambiguous change. The motive was to enable the powerful to acquire land from their poorer neighbours as well as to raise productivity. It is not obvious that productivity per acre was always raised, not immediately anyhow.

These summary remarks are not intended to imply that northern farmers failed to take advantage of the new crops and methods. They did so aggressively once there were northern industrial cities to supply. But in general southern arable farming was more progressive, or more progressive earlier, in line with the advantages of proximity to the London market, sources of continental ideas, and a more conducive ecological setting. Enterprise in the south was far from lacking but did not find local industry as rewarding as farming and the associated service trades. Accordingly, when capital was productively invested in the south, it tended to go into agriculture, to be recouped from farm rents. In addition the region allocated capital and talent to the agricultural processing trades, milling, malting and brewing, which were means of reducing the weight and bulk of crops before conveying them to market (cattle and sheep were moved on the hoof). Moving produce to the main markets inspired investment in transport and communications. The services of solicitors and bankers facilitated all these profitable tasks. The results may be seen in the fine Georgian houses of the market towns that ring the capital, such as Newbury, Abingdon and Henley, all riverside towns. In contrast little fresh capital entered southern manufacturing. Industrial plant hung on only until some accident befell it – a fire, the breaking of a mill dam - after which it was seldom replaced.

7 Technology and specialization
The achievements of the specialized communities of little watch and clock manufacturers in the north-west were seldom noticed by the rich opinion-formers of London. A large number of their products survive from the seventeenth and eighteenth centuries and the many improvements in design have been closely studied and admired. Some of these are mentioned in surviving documents (for

example at the Royal Society) so that innovators like Tompion and Graham have become famous.[58] The names on the dials of clocks and watches are often those of fashionable 'makers' in London or the country towns. In many cases probably the only contribution of these 'makers', apart from effecting repairs, was to put together the major parts – the movement, the dial, and the case – and test the whole before selling it.[59]

There are virtually no archives to identify the Lancashire workers who improved the manufacturing techniques. Prices and surviving instruments are the sole evidence of an extraordinary leap in manufacturing productivity. Adam Smith noted that a watch costing £20 in the mid-seventeenth century was 95 per cent cheaper by 1776 (i.e. cost only £1 in 1776) and was better made too.[60] There is only one patent but this does not seem to have advanced horology.[61]

Yet in almost every discussion of early spinning machinery inventors and their patents are given the prime position and their contribution has been thought to deserve renown. In reality the technical problems of devising cotton-spinning machinery were modest and less difficult than many horological conundrums. The main obstacles to the development of spinning machines were social. In 1750 there were probably about 20,000 full-time spinners in Lancashire and many part-timers as well. It was widely recognized that it would not be acceptable to put large numbers of these people out of work. In the 1730s, when the manufacture of cotton started to increase, Paul and Wyatt made spinning machines but never dared take them to Lancashire.[62] Without the help of experienced Lancastrian cotton spinners they were unable to get them to work successfully.[63] James Taylor, a clock-maker of Ashton-under-Lyne, Lancashire, got a patent in 1754 (No 693) but decided not to make machines. Thomas Highs of Leigh,

---

[58] Landes, 1983 pp 114 - 157.
[59] Campbell, 1747 pp 250 - 252.
[60] Smith, 1776, Book 1, Ch XI, Part 3, p 243.
[61] No 344 of 1695.
[62] Patents Nos 562, June 1738, 636, Aug 1748, 724, June 1758.
[63] Wadswoth & Mann, 1931, pp 419 - 448; Hills, 1970, pp 32 - 52.

Lancashire, experimented in 1763-1765 but also decided not to proceed.[64] Some of Hargreaves' machines were destroyed.[65] He and Arkwright went to Nottingham, where no cotton spinning was done, in order to get their patents and set up factories in 1769-1770.[66]

Strutt and Need of Nottingham bought half of Arkwright's patent and spent £13,000 perfecting the machinery and installing it in a water-mill at Cromford, Derbyshire, which produced a yarn ideal for hosiery and for replacing the linen warp in cotton cloth. The new cloth that was made with it was much better for printing, which helped to accelerate the production of printed cottons. Hargreaves was unable to enforce his patent because he had previously sold machines.

Two factors were important in the rapid adoption of mechanization. First, the many small manufacturers were able to persuade their workers to use the new machinery. The demand for cotton cloth expanded so rapidly that no spinners seem to have become unemployed. Another factor was that their pay was much increased. In 1780 a House of Commons Committee was told that 'one person [on a jenny] can manufacture as much cotton yarn as nine persons can do by hand' … 'and can now get 2s to 2s 6d [24 – 30 pence] a day.' They also learnt that 'sixteen years earlier (i.e. in 1764) a woman could earn from ten to fifteen pence per day by the single spindle'.[67] The common wage of women in the area between 1760 and 1780 was only 6d – 9d a day. The significance of this can be seen by comparing it with the troubles in getting wool spinners to use the new machinery in the West of England.[68] Secondly, the manufacturers and other 'ingenious mechanics' were able to make many improvements to jennies. By 1775 a better machine was being illustrated in America. By 1788 there were

---

[64] Fitton, 1989, p 14.

[65] Aspin, 1970, pp 120 - 1.

[66] Arkwright Patent 931 July 1769; Hargreaves Patent 962 June 1770.

[67] Journal House of Commons, vol 37, pp 195-6.

[68] Mann, 1971, pp 123 - 135.

20,070 jennies in use.[69] Crompton worked on one and it was his new ideas that proved particularly fertile. The consequences of mechanization in the cotton industry were therefore stunning but it is appropriate to look for their deep sources in the watch and clock and tool making trades.

The general principle that had guided the watch and clock industry was that the more people who had a chance to improve the techniques of manufacturing, the better and the quicker good answers to problems would be found. This principle also applied to cotton spinning. The north-west had plenty of craftsmen with a little capital so their society proved particularly suitable for this type of experimentation. But by the 1770s the society also contained some larger capitalists who were willing to risk their money on the bigger projects, such as water-powered machinery, canals and steam engines, which became part of the dense structure of north-western manufacturing.

Technological change also occurred in the south, which was not quite an industrial desert, but the density of the business culture in the north had the advantage. In London there was a great deal of small-scale workshop industry making consumer goods, but the tendency to abandon manufactures of lesser value to the provinces may have meant that economies of scale in mass production were lost.

8 Conclusions
Innumerable explanations of industrialization have been advanced. So many variables were changing at the same period that almost none has escaped being treated as the one true key to change. What might be termed 'coal determinism' is especially hard to eradicate. Among background conditions, however, were the following: the optimism associated with the Enlightenment; the acceptance of market ideology; and the shift of intra-elite competition from political and religious spheres towards economics and commerce, meaning from zero-sum to non-zero sum. These abstractions

---

[69] Aspin & Chapman, 1964, pp 48 - 9 (but incorrectly quotes the Journal of the House of Commons mentioned above) & Plate 1 opposite p 45.

describe the context and are advances on the single-factor approaches commonly put forward, but they are still incomplete. Neither new habits of thought nor laws and institutions fully account for the expansion and deepening of the economy. They are particularly weak when it comes to explaining the shifting distributions of economic activity.

Legal scholars do not find the law, and even less the way the law was administered, an adequate explanation of growth. There are too many ambiguities. In some respects the judges appeared market-friendly, for instance in dismantling elements of guild power, as they had started to do as early as 1599. In other respects they declined to lift traditional restrictions, for instance those on the marketing of grain. They did not trust the market to supply the poor and had the preservation of social order in mind. Property rights often remained vaguely described and ill-defined. This was Max Weber's 'England Problem'; he was perplexed that growth initially occurred in a country where rights were so uncertain they might have been expected to deter any prudent investor.[70]

What Weber noted was much to the point. Recent adulatory work, eagerly embraced by many in the economics profession, celebrates 1688 as the start of security for property, supposedly conferring a first mover advantage on England. Yet it has not been shown that the supposed absence of secure rights before the Glorious Revolution actually deterred investment, for this was clearly on the rise during the 1650s and 1660s. In any case many rights remained contestable and in some spheres remained thoroughly archaic in form well into Victorian times. Although it is clearly an exception, the ancient practice of transferring land via the ceremony of 'turf and twig' survives with respect to Kings Heath at Malmesbury, Wiltshire - land that was given to the men of the borough by King Athelstan. Of course it is an exception, but it is the exception that proves the rule. Nevertheless, while the legal system moved sluggishly and lacked clarity, it was adaptable. The solutions to disputes about ownership were often achieved by negotiation, not necessarily involving written contracts, and owed more to practice

---

[70] Heller, 2009, pp 19 & 103.

than to theory. The power of the market in a creative, broadly-based economy was sufficient to bypass particular difficulties over property rights and their enforcement.

Rich northerners absorbed the culture of the gentry when they came south but they brought with them their high ethical standards - honesty in government as in business, an abhorrence of corruption and a belief in promotion on merit in government service. Their standards avoided the corruption that heavily burdened many affairs until the national 'clean up' in the second quarter of the nineteenth century. Despite all impediments, therefore, both private and public investment expanded. Southerners meanwhile specialized not only in the agricultural sector but also in naval and military affairs and overseas trade.

Growth was regionally expressed yet few textbook explanations emphasize regional change. Customary offerings purport to be national in scope whereas in reality industrialization should be understood as a regional, even local, phenomenon. The emergence and self-propelled intensification of the business culture in the north-west is a realistic explanation, contrasting as it did with the allocation of talent away from manufacturing in the south. This gradual bifurcation took place within an increasingly integrated national market that rewarded scale and specialization.

The chain of events and processes leading to industrialization included the manner in which small farmers in the north-west were able to acquire some capital during the 'rent revolution' of the sixteenth century. It involved their puritanism, non-conformity, thrift and enterprise, and the way they compensated for deficiencies in their resource endowment by importing raw materials lacking in their district. At times they were fortunate to be aided by exogenous events or politically successful lobbying: the opening for their cheese when the herds of the Suffolk dairymen were hit by disease, the protection of the sail-cloth industry that grew up around Warrington, changes in the salt tax favouring their rock salt, and so forth. Businesses in the north-west presumably gained inadvertently from, though they did not cause, the industrial decay of southern England. That process reflected the alternative attraction of growing cereals for the London food market, as well as the tendency for men to aspire to the gentry class, which the non-conformist businessmen of the north-west had often managed to resist. The sense of purpose and interconnected manufactures of the north-west gave rise to the further innovations on which mass production came to rest.

Part II

Wealth distribution and wealth creation in societies manufacturing cotton in Europe - Italy, Germany, Lancashire and Holland 1100-1789

Charles F Foster

1 Introduction

It is generally agreed that between 1750 and 1850 the world entered a new phase in its economic life in which the wealth of large numbers of people, particularly Europeans, increased to an extent that was unimaginable to people in the three thousand years between say 1500 BC and 1500 AD. For the last 25 years I have researched and written about economic life in North-West England in the 16th, 17th and 18th centuries. This has led me to that most intriguing but also vexing of questions: why did the Industrial Revolution come about when and where it did, in the 18th century, in England, with much of the action centred on the North-West?

One of the most telling displays of the sheer size of the change wrought on the world by that revolution is a table derived from a series which appears in Angus Maddison's 2007 book, *Contours of the World Economy*. This table (see page 40) shows that in 1700 the gross domestic product in Western Europe was just under $1000 *per capita* (in 1990 International dollars - Table 1) but that by 2003 it was a little under $20,000. It also shows that in AD 1000 Europeans had the same standard of living as all the rest of the world's population - a *per capita* income of around $450. According to Maddison's figures the difference between the Europeans and the rest of the world began to appear between 1000 and 1500 when West European income increased by about 80% to $771. The suggestion of this essay is that the driving forces for this change were technical and commercial innovations. The North Italian city states were the leaders in this change and their ability to innovate is linked here to the wide distribution of wealth that empowered so many of their citizens. If this analysis is correct it was the maintenance of this type of society in at least some parts of Europe for several centuries that caused the development of

Western Europe to be so different from that of other continents. It may be that the example of a society with greater economic equality was one of Europe's principal gifts to the peoples of the world.

Maddison's sweeping world view from 1 AD to the present day forms a framework for the three detailed examples of societies where wealth was created which form the body of this essay. Three factors emerge as important for wealth creation - wealth distribution, technical and commercial innovation and plural political institutions. The three are linked together. A wide distribution of wealth ensures that a large number of families own a small amount of capital. Only a few people in each generation are innovators and each needs a bit of capital to give them the time to experiment and to make the prototypes of their innovation, whether this is a physical object or a scheme for a new type of trading. It would seem that it is only when there are plenty of families with some capital that there is a steady flow of innovators bringing their ideas to fruition. Societies in which many people own some capital seem also to be societies with plural political institutions. A large number of capitalists demand a share in creating laws at national, regional and local level. They also require to play a part in enforcing those laws and deciding the penalties that should be imposed on law-breakers. Parliaments and juries are well known features of plural political institutions. Such institutions, of course, normally seek to maintain the positions of those who elect the members of parliaments and serve on juries and so they protect the capital of small owners. In this way the three factors form a self-sustaining social system.

But among those who possess money there are usually some who want to increase their own wealth by altering the laws and customs of their society to their own advantage, or perhaps just to prevent the changes - such as those caused by higher taxes - which will ensure a more equal society. If such people are successful in their political activity they may transform a previously fairly plural society into an oligarchy or perhaps even into a monarchy or dictatorship. As wealth is concentrated in fewer hands, rich people may reorder the political institutions of their society so that they gain even more power and with it the ability to direct even more wealth to themselves.

The subject of wealth distribution has not had much attention from economic historians. One of the reasons is that suitable archives are scarce. The origin of my section on Lancashire was my discovery of the tax returns of 1543-5, the rare lists of the Poll Taxes and the Hearth Taxes of the 1660s, and the surveys and valuations that revealed how they could be used to show wealth distribution. It appeared that there was probably a connection between Lancashire's wealth distribution and the development of cotton-spinning machinery there in the 1770. This played a large role in the Industrial Revolution. This set me looking for any archives that would reveal wealth distribution in the two European societies that had manufactured cotton cloth before Lancashire - Italy and South Germany. My discoveries in this area resulted in the present essay.

In all three of the examples I have selected we see a large number of families acquiring some capital as a result of changes in population and in political and economic circumstances which they themselves had not caused. In the first example these newly enriched families, spread across the northern half of Italy, created many innovations and much wealth over perhaps three and a half centuries (1000 - 1350). In the last of these centuries wealth became more concentrated in the families who had been most successful in business and in politics. The original plural government became more oligarchic and the ability of the society to innovate to meet new challenges declined, along with its ability to continue to increase its wealth. In the second society (South Germany 1370 - 1520) the creative period was much shorter because the survivors of the 'old rich' recovered their old political position and took control of the wealth again. In the third example (Lancashire 1400 - 1800) the society continued to be plural and innovative throughout the whole period examined and indeed continued to be creative into the next century, although wealth in this last period became increasingly the birth-right of families who were successful in business. Towards the end of the 19th century that generated such a lot of political protest that in the first 80 years of the 20th century wealth was redistributed much more widely again by high taxation and the control of rents.

A fourth area is given rather less attention - the Netherlands 1400 - 1800. Due to its geographical position in the centre of 'business Europe' it developed in the early stages, both technically and commercially, much faster than Lancashire. But after 1700 most wealth accumulated in the hands of a small oligarchy and there was little innovation from then on.

Table 1   Per capita GDP 1 – 2003 AD
(1990 International dollars)

	AD 1	1000	1500	1600	1700	1820	2003
Belgium	450	425	875	976	1,144	1,319	21,205
France	473	425	727	841	910	1,135	21,861
Germany	408	410	688	791	910	1,077	19,144
Italy	809	450	1,100	1,100	1,100	1,117	19,151
Netherlands	425	425	761	1,381	2,130	1,838	21,480
UK	400	400	714	974	1,250	1,706	21,310
W. European average	576	427	771	889	997	1,202	19,912
Egypt	600	550	500	500	500	500	3,034
Iran/Iraq	500	650	575	575	575	588	3,300
Japan	400	425	500	520	570	669	21,218
India	450	450	550	550	550	533	2,160
China	450	450	600	600	600	600	4,803
Africa	472	425	414	422	421	420	6,549

Source: Maddison, A., 2007, Tables A,7,4,3,4,12 and 6.6.
Countries selected to illustrate the present book.

Maddison's tables use a technique that he and others developed when he was working for the OECD to convert the money values of different periods and different countries into a single series. This technique made use of a concept which they named 'purchasing power parity'.   In these tables the figures are expressed in 1990 International Dollars. In his book he noted that it was a common feature in early societies for all the wealth to be concentrated in a small group who controlled the government, the military and often the Church. He provided an example of such a society - the Roman Empire. The Emperor was head of the civil government, top general and also chief Priest. He and the senators owned large estates in peninsular Italy and controlled the Empire. Wealth in the peninsula averaged $875 per capita, but was under $500 in almost all the rest of the Empire. There was a well-organized army, large buildings and good roads, but little technical innovation.

The three factors involved in wealth creation, discussed on p 38 above, are very general. New wealth is created by activities like the introduction of new plants or new agricultural equipment, by more trading activities and so on. The link between these practical changes and the broad principles may sometimes be hard to find but they probably exist. For example, by 1000 AD, as shown in Table 1, the Roman Empire had collapsed and all Europe was as poor as ever it had been. The new rich empire was that of the Abbasid Caliphs in Baghdad. According to Watson they made large improvements in irrigating land and in water-lifting technology, especially in Iraq. New crops were introduced, such as sugar, cotton and rice.[1] The caliphs encouraged scholarship and advances were made in astronomy, mathematics and medicine[2] but their society failed to develop a capacity for continual growth. Was this because the Caliphs and their courtiers were themselves too rich and powerful?

This essay is divided into seven sections which follow the progress of cotton manufacture which began in Europe after 1100, and, in the process, it examines the distribution of wealth, the character of the political institutions and the progress of wealth creation. Section 2 covers the North Italian cities from 1000 to 1500; Section 3 covers South Germany from about 1300 to 1600. In

---

[1] Watson, 1983, pp 15 & following; Decker, 2009, suggests that this thesis is exaggerated.
[2] Maddison, 2007, pp 189-93.

Section 4 the progress of European wealth creation between 1000 and 1600 is briefly reviewed by reference to Table 1. Section 5 deals with Lancashire, 1600 – 1700. Section 6 describes the European reaction to the import of a substantial quantity of Indian cottons between 1670 and 1720 and makes a detailed analysis of the development of cotton-spinning machines in the period 1768-1785. This was one of the decisive moments in the growth of European wealth creation. Complex production machinery, which replaced the labour of first, tens of thousands, then hundreds of thousands and finally millions of people, was a completely new phenomenon. Our great wealth today is largely based on technical improvements of this kind – for example we email messages around the world instead of posting letters. Section 7 briefly shows how the Netherlands failed to maintain in the 18th century its outstanding growth rate of the previous centuries and summarizes the growth in wealth creation in Europe until 1820.

2 North Italian cities 1000 – 1500
Cotton cultivation was probably introduced to Europe by Islamic settlers to Sicily and southern Spain in the 9th and 10th centuries but its use seems not to have spread beyond these Muslim communities. The 10th and 11th centuries saw the break-up of the great Italian ecclesiastical estates and the weakening of Carolingian Imperial authority. In a most unusual social development, between two and three hundred towns in the northern half of Italy became more or less independent political entities by the early 12th century. What appears to have happened is that townsmen started trading more actively and became rich enough to enclose their town with a wall. Families living in the town usually owned most of the land in the surrounding district which provided their food supply. Some of the richer families claimed to be noble but almost all engaged in trade. Because of the weakness of lay and ecclesiastical princes, who were seeking supporters, the towns were able to negotiate political freedoms.

Before 1100 Venice, Genoa, and Pisa, which had the best harbours among the North Italian towns, had competed successfully with the Byzantines for trade in the Mediterranean, and were importing the spices, dried fruits, jewels, and luxury textiles which were popular with kings and noblemen. The Crusades transformed the position by establishing a West European state in the Middle East. With the First Crusade of 1096-9 North Italian merchants gained access to the coastal towns of the Levant. While the crusader knights were principally interested in acquiring estates with rent and tax-paying tenants, the business-minded North Italians realized the potential of the Islamic technology in silk and cotton manufacture and in dyeing skills. They brought the fibres and the knowledge of how to use them and how to dye them back to Venice and Genoa. Silk and cotton fibres, with the dyestuffs and mordants to colour both them and wool, were well known in the Islamic world, but were mostly new to Western Europe.[3] The manufacture and export of these new textiles generated much of the wealth that made Northern Italy the economic power house of Europe in the period 1100 to 1500.

Cotton fibre was being imported into Venice by 1125, as is shown by surviving Venetian documents.[4] Italian women learnt how to spin a soft coarse yarn from cotton that was suitable for weft. However it was evidently impossible to find people to spin from cotton the strongly twisted yarn required for the warp, so they decided to use their native linen. For the next six centuries cotton cloth made in Europe normally consisted of a linen warp and a cotton weft. These mixed-fibre cloths were called *pignolati* and *fustagni*, the latter being the origin of the English word fustian. The weaker cotton weft could be thickly woven around the warp, producing a soft dense fabric. Cotton was much easier to dye than linen and the dense, coloured weft often covered the undyed warp threads in the finished material. The Po valley was a region where the processing of linen from locally grown flax and hemp was already well established, so it soon became the area which provided the linen warp threads for fustians. Cotton manufacture spread westwards from Venice to Padua and Verona, while from Genoa it moved inland and eastwards to Piacenza, Cremona, Pavia, and Milan, and along the coast to the south of France. By the 1140s cotton cloth was being exported from Italy to Jerusalem, Constantinople and Alexandria, and before the end of the century it

---

[3] Mazzaoui, 1981, pp 17-24, 93-6.
[4] Mazzaoui, 1981, p 29.

was being sold all over Europe. It was a cheap, mass-produced product. Very little seems to be known about the amount produced in these early centuries but by 1348 there may have been between 6,000 and 9,000 cotton workers in Milan.[5]

The silk industry developed more slowly and settled in the area around Lucca, using raw silk imported into neighbouring Pisa, and a silk-throwing mill powered by water. This outstanding invention was apparently developed in Lucca around 1200 and used in only a few North Italian cities.[6] This machine spun the highest quality silk and so gave Italy a dominant position in the silk market for centuries. It was not until 1718 that the machine was copied and taken to England by the Lombe brothers. This example shows that the Italians had substantial innovative skills, enabling them to adapt eastern designs and modify the foreign technology for their own populations.

The third textile for which Italy became famous in this period was woollen cloth. This too was concentrated in its own area – the hill towns of Tuscany and Umbria, of which Florence became the largest and most famous. The Tuscan hills had supported sheep for centuries and Florence had its own fulling mill by 1062,[7] but its woollen cloth was low quality and sold only to locals. The first change seems to have been that, around 1200, Florentine dyers began to 'refinish' the more expensive cloths that were being imported into Genoa from Flanders.[8] By the middle of the 13th century wool was being imported into North Italy and better quality cloth was being manufactured. Around 1300 about 100,000 cloths were being made annually in Florence. By the 1330s the quality had been improved again, apparently with the new Languedoc method of carding and wheel-spinning the weft.[9] From the 1340s onwards 70,000 – 80,000 pieces of cloth were made yearly, each worth about 15 florins, making a total value of 1.2m florins.[10]

---

[5] Mazzaoui, 1981, pp 29, 62-5, & 113, note 40.
[6] CIBA Review No. 80 (1950).
[7] CIBA Review No. 1 (1937).
[8] Pullan, 1973, p. 100. Chorley, 1987, p 352.
[9] Chorley, 1997, pp 10-12.
[10] Cipolla, 1976, quoting Cronica Villani, pp 194 – 5.

The amazing expansion of textile manufacture and the extraordinary development of business in North Italy before 1330 can be approximately gauged from the size of the populations that grew up in its towns. By 1330 Genoa, Venice, Milan and Florence are each thought to have attained about 100,000 inhabitants. Siena had perhaps 45,000, Pisa 38,000 and Padua about 30,000.[11] Probably the most important reason for the popularity of cloth made in northern Italy was the superior quality of the dyeing and finishing techniques which had been learnt in the Levant, but hugely improved and extended by the innovative people working in the North Italian towns. The spread of Italian merchants across the whole of Europe and the Middle East in the 13th to 15th centuries, and the many innovations they made in accounting, money transmission and banking, have been noticed by many historians. It has been called "a kind of 'business Civilization'".[12] This activity was all firmly based on the Italians' commanding position in textiles, both those imported from the Islamic world and those manufactured in Italy.

How can we account for the appearance of this extraordinarily vigorous business society? What exactly happened and what caused it to happen? Early archives from the Po valley towns seem to be scarce but Pistoia, a town in the hills just south of the centre of the Po valley, 37km north-west of Florence, has one of the best collections of early archives, and David Herlihy has provided an exemplary guide to them, so I will take it as my example.[13]

The town of Pistoia is in the centre of a fertile valley in the hills, at the point where five main roads converge. The area of the saucer, including most of the hills, is about 900 sq kms. Herlihy estimates that in the year 1100 about 30% of the population were serfs of the Bishop and another 10% were serfs of three great titled families. The remaining 60% were *valvassores, cattoni, castellani* or

---

[11] Pullan, 1973, p. 117; Cipolla, 1976, p. 281; Herlihy, 1958, p. 36; Waley, 1991, p 26.

[12] Jones, 1973, p 11.

[13] Herlihy, 1967.

lambardi' whom he calls petty nobles, and who seem to have been similar to the people we meet in England known as charterers or freeholders. They probably originally held their small farms in return for military service to a far away Emperor. The population of northern Italy seems to have expanded in the relatively peaceful times after the year 1000 and the rising prices of both food and land are likely to have put capital into the hands of old established families and allowed them to engage more extensively in trade. Their lands were divided into over 100 communes (or townships), of which the town of Pistoia was one. In 1105 two consuls appear for the first time at the head of the government of the town. The importance there of trading is shown by the record of its steadily growing control over the five roads that led to it. The military background of the citizens was reflected in their duty to serve in the town's army, with nobles serving as its cavalry. It was this ability to put armies in the field that enabled the Italian Communes to win political independence.

So, from 1100 onwards, we see Pistoia as a town of self-governing small businessmen, slowly expanding its jurisdiction over all the land in its saucer of hills. By the first half of the 13th century it had completed the task and in 1244 counted all the hearths in its territory so that it could tax them.[14] This Book of Hearths listed 7,049 commoner hearths and 263 noble ones in 124 communes. Herlihy estimated this rural population at 34,000 and that of the city at the same time as around 11,000. Rural taxes were collected in Italy at this period in the same way as the Land Tax was collected in England until 1800. The central authorities allotted a quota to every commune which then divided it among the householders. Only the local people knew who owned the land and how valuable it was.

A tax return for Piuvica, the third largest commune in Pistoia, survives for 1243. Piuvica was a village in the rich arable plain, 5km south of the city of Pistoia. The return lists 238 resident householders and the Book of Hearths tells us that there were also 24 nobles who owned houses there, and lived part of the time there,

---

[14] Herlihy, 1967, pp 30-2.

paying their taxes in the city. The wide distribution of wealth is shown in Table 2.

Table 2 The distribution of wealth in the Commune of Piuvica in 1243[15]

	Number of householders	% of total		% Wealth of Commune
The richest	24	10	owned	32.10
The next richest	24	10	owned	17.90
The next richest	24	10	owned	14.00
The next richest	24	10	owned	10.50
The next richest	24	10	owned	7.20
so the richest	120	50	owned	81.70
and the poorest	118	50	owned	18.30
Totals	238	100		100

As we shall see in other tables below, to have as large a group as 50 per cent of the householders controlling 80% of the wealth of a community was an unusually equal distribution. Herlihy, in presenting this table, has drawn attention to 'the importance of the middle level of this social pyramid' which he believes 'may justifiably be called a rural middle class'.[16] It is also true that in the middle of the 13th century the better-off citizens in the rural areas were rapidly moving into the city to take part in the exciting growth of business. The Book of Hearths tells us that 13 of Piuvica's residents had moved to the city since the tax return of the previous year. This movement of the richer citizens seems to have been common in northern Italy and is confirmed by the research of J. Plesner.[17] So whereas the country areas had earlier been filled with small property owners and the rural householders had been accustomed to paying, on average, twice as much tax as city

---

[15] Herlihy, 1967, p 183.
[16] Herlihy, 1967, p 183.
[17] Herlihy, 1967, p 184.

families, that ceased to be equitable after the rich landowners moved into the city. By 1300 the Pistoian authorities gave up trying to collect tax in the old way.[18] To cope with this situation the Venetians had developed a new tax called the *Catasto* (cadastre in English). In this system, which spread throughout northern Italy, the city authorities made all citizens declare their wealth in great detail, and it was all recorded in ledgers so that everyone knew that the tax burden was fairly divided.

This leads to our next evidence of wealth distibution, the *Catasto* of Orvieto in 1292. Orvieto was a medium sized town built on a precipitous crag in the middle of the upper Tiber valley. Like many successful northern towns it had expanded its territory, so that the Commune included substantial rural lands, a number of smaller towns and villages, and the estates and castles of nobles. The town had a woollen and a cotton industry and a population of about 20,000. Waley has suggested this cadastre may be characteristic of an inland town at this period.[19]

---

[18] Herlihy, 1967, pp 183-5 & 233.
[19] Waley, 1969, p 24.

Table 3 Approximate wealth of householders in Orvieto in 1292

Number	%	cum. %	average wealth (lira)	range of wealth (lira)	total wealth of group (lira)	%	cum. %
34	1.2		12,501	5,855 - 33,925	425,057	20.1	
191	6.7	7.9	3,600	2,000 - 7,819	687,729	32.6	52.7
244	8.6	16.5	say 1,500	1,000 - 2,000	366,000	17.3	70
371	13.1	29.6	say 750	500 - 1,000	278,250	13.2	83.2
1,031	36.3	65.9	say 300	100 - 500	309,300	14.6	97.8
442 }	} 34.1	100	say 75	50 - 100	33,150 }	} 2.2	100
528 }	}		say 25	up to 50	13,200 }	}	
__2,841__					__2,112,686__		

Notes
1. *Figures from Pardi, 1896,* Il Catasto.
2. *These assessments were made on householders' lands and possessions in the whole city-state. The householders living in the* contado - *the towns, castles and villages in the rest of the Commune's territory - were separately assessed.*
3. *The richest 34 men were from 24 families and included 3 counts.*
4. *Orvieto used the lira of Cortona. In 1292 1000 Lira Cortonese was equal to 430 gold florins and this weight of gold was then worth approx. £57 sterling.*[20]

---

[20] Spufford, 1986, p 57.

This cadastre probably included most of the nobles and other well-off families in the city-state of Orvieto so it was a different type of community from the group of resident small landowners in Piuvica. It can be seen that the distribution of wealth in Orvieto, with 52.7% of the wealth in the hands of 7.9% of households, was not as wide as that in Piuvica. But there was still a significant spread, with 29% of households controlling 83.29% of the wealth.

In their most dynamic period, 1050-1300, most of the North Italian city-states were at first governed by elected consuls. These often gave way to large councils with many subcommittees. The laws and the courts were structured to support the business activities that many of them were engaged in – for example business ledgers were accepted as evidence of payments. In these business communities reformist religious groups such as the Cathars, the Umiliati, the Waldensians and the mendicant Franciscan friars sprang up. The doctrines of Peter Valdes, a merchant of Lyons, were condemned by the Council of Verona in 1184 and Francis, son of a merchant of Assisi, was born in 1181. All these groups stressed the importance of ordinary people and their hard work.[21] Taxes were raised only to fund communal purposes, like the repair of the walls or improvements to the water supply.

As town populations grew city government also had to change. The committees of leading citizens gave way to new Chief Magistrates, called *Podesta*. Elected for a short spell of years, these new rulers often came from the families of the great landed nobility. Whatever their route to power, some of them succeeded in making the office permanent and hereditary in their families, so that after 1300 the North Italian cities were increasingly controlled by '*Signori*'. Whereas the groups of merchants had aimed to increase the wealth and well-being of their fellow citizens, a *signor* might seek good dynastic marriages for his children or to enlarge the territories of his 'possession'. In pursuit of these objectives wars were waged and taxes raised. The budgets of the towns mushroomed. For example, the annual expenditure of the

---

[21] Pullan, 1973, pp 64-70.

Commune of Siena in 1226 was only 6,300 Lira; by 1328 this had increased to 347,000 Lira.[22]

A small army of officials came into existence to administer the new taxes. They were much assisted by the existence of cadastres but the ruler also needed political support. This was often achieved by an alliance with the local nobility and also with the principal merchants. The well established Guild system of the towns was subverted and deftly manipulated to the advantage of the ruling family. For example, in 1260, in one brilliant stroke, the incoming *Signor* in Verona, Mastino della Scala, assumed the title '*Podesta*' of the House of Merchants, so concentrating in himself both economic and political control of the city.[23] To resist the growing power of the rich, often referred to as magnates, the less wealthy, middle class citizens in some towns joined together in political groups which became known as the '*popolo*'. In the second half of the 13th century such groups often wielded considerable power[24] but for many reasons they mostly succumbed to the *Signori* in the 14th century. During that century there were great changes in North Italian towns. The Black Death and other plagues and famines affected the tightly packed urban communities even more than the rest of rural Europe. Herlihy has brilliantly unravelled the course of events near Pistoia. He lists 32 years between 1313 and 1458 when there was either famine or plague in the town. The problems of providing food, clean water, and sanitation for the huge urban populations proved insuperable. Populations fell dramatically - Florence from over 100,000 in 1330 to 37,000 in 1427, and Pisa, on a less healthy site, from 38,000 to 7,333.[25] As we have seen, many rural property owners had moved into the city in the second half of the 13th century. They let their lands to tenants at full market rents. As the population increased before 1313, the prices of food of all kinds rose, tenants made profits, and rents moved higher. As populations fell in the 14th century, food

---

[22] Waley, 1991, p. 79. In gold the value of the 1328 lira was about a quarter of the value of the 1226 lira.

[23] Mazzaoui, 1981, p 124.

[24] Waley, 1981, pp 45-7, 101-4.

[25] Herlihy, 1958, p 37, Herlihy & Klapisch-Zuber, 1985, pp 67-9.

prices fell faster than rents and the capital of tenant farmers was destroyed. Most of the land near cities came to be cultivated by share-croppers on '*mezzadria*' leases, where the worker owned nothing. As well as the land itself, the land-owner provided the tools, the seed and the animals, while the tenant was not infrequently saddled with a load of debt he could never repay. Well-off city dwellers increasingly became rentiers and business declined.[26]

Between 1200 and 1400 other slow changes came over Italian towns. Originally their culture seems to have consistently favoured business. However the make-up of the city population gradually changed. As the cities became richer and their armies became more powerful the nobles were persuaded that their estates would be better protected if they joined the city and agreed to live part of the year there. The increasing number of nobles living in the towns had other effects. Serfs had largely disappeared from North Italy because the egalitarian culture of the towns had always refused to accept serfdom. But now the rich, high-status nobles imported their military culture into the cities. Fighting between rival families became endemic and resort to war was more natural. Nobles easily accepted the government of *Signori* – indeed they often aspired to be the *Signor* themselves. Townsmen began to regard craft and mercantile activities as menial occupations which excluded them from the upper classes.[27] The impact of these changes on the distribution of wealth can be seen from a short analysis of the great *Catasto* of Florence in 1427.[28]

---

[26] Herlihy, 1967, pp 121-137.
[27] Cipolla, 1976, p 236.
[28] Herlihy, Klapisch-Zuber, Litchfield and Molho, *Online Catasto*.

Table 4   Wealth distribution in the City of Florence and the Florentine State in 1427.

City of Florence

Range of taxable wealth (florins)	No of households	%	Cum. %	Total taxable wealth (florins)	%	Cum. %
10,000 - 101,000	101	1		2,115,134	27.5	
2,000 - 9,999	733	7.4	8.4	2,908,289	37.9	65.4
1,000 - 1,999	818	8.2	16.6	1,159,980	15.1	80.5
500 - 999	1,080	10.8	27.4	773,402	10.1	90.6
200 - 499	1,519	15.3	42.7	499,271	6.5	97.1
10 - 199	2,354	23.7	66.4	222,628	2.9	100
0 - 9	3,341	33.6	100	683	0	100
Totals	**9,946**			**7,679,387**		

Florentine State

Range of taxable wealth (florins)	No of households	%	Cum. %	Total taxable wealth (florins)	%	Cum. %
10,000 - 101,000	108	0.17		2,182,698	18.5	
2,000 - 9,999	847	1.4	1.6	3,281,785	27.8	46.3
1,000 - 1,999	1,089	1.8	3.4	1,523,826	12.9	59.2
500 - 999	1,969	3.2	6.6	1,371,961	11.6	70.8
200 - 499	4,883	8.1	14.7	1,514,474	12.8	83.6
10 - 199	32,043	53	67.7	1,874,366	15.9	99.5
0 - 9	19,542	32.3	100	33,226	0.3	99.8
Totals	**60,481**			**11,782,336**		

Notes.
1. The differences between the figures here and various printed texts, eg Herlihy and Klapisch-Zuber, Tuscans, p 94, are due to researchers correcting errors in the originals. They are not significant.
2. In 1427 200 gold florins was equal to approx. £34 sterling.

The Florentine state in 1427, with its 60,000 households, was much larger than the City of Orvieto in 1292, with only 2,841 households (see Table 3), and the difference in wealth distribution is also striking. In the Florentine state just 14.7% of households owned 83.6% of the wealth, compared with the 29.6% in Orvieto in 1292 who owned 83.2%. Part of the reason for the difference is that the Orvieto figures cover only the residents of the town itself and an area of about 5 kilometres around it who owned land, whereas the Florentine figures include households having any kind of wealth, of whom about 62% lived in rural areas. However, if we compare the Orvieto figures only with the households living within the walls of the city of Florence, we find that 16.6% of urban Florentines owned 80.5% of the wealth in 1427, which is still about half the percentage in Orvieto 135 years earlier. There is no doubting the great concentration of wealth that has occurred. In 1427 only 8,896 Florentine households had significant capital and 4,251 of them lived in the city of Florence itself. The rich Florentines in 1427 were much richer than the rich Orvietans had been in 1292. The 37,000 families living in the country areas were nearly all poor. This great concentration of wealth in a small number of urban families is of course what enabled the creation of the amazing art-works of the Italian Renaissance.

The position we observed in Piuvica in 1243, of property-owning families resident in the country, each paying twice as much tax on average as city families, had been completely reversed by 1427. Rich residents in the city owned most of the land and paid most of the tax. It is not surprising that the government of the North Italian towns had evolved from one in which many citizens took part to one controlled by a small oligarchy. The vigour and innovative character of Italian business ebbed away after 1300 but a great quantity of technical expertise and business organization, which was not replicated elsewhere in Europe, remained, so that the textile industry did not die quickly. There was a movement from the over-regulated towns to the less regulated countryside.[29] But by 1700 an exporting textile industry in Italy barely existed and the country was no longer rich.

3   South Germany 1300 - 1600
It is likely that the great expansion of textile manufacturing in northern Italy in the 13th century created a scarcity of workers. South German merchants distributing Italian cottons north of the Alps must have seen an opportunity to organize local manufacture. The first record of raw cotton crossing the Alps is dated 1282.[30] The merchants were mainly based in three Swabian towns - Augsburg, Ulm, and Memmingen - all important distribution points north of the Alpine passes. German towns at this period were

---

[29] Mazzaoui, 1981, pp 152-3, Sella, 1979, pp 87 & 113-4.
[30] Mazzaoui, 1981, p 139.

small, similar to Italian towns before 1100. However, from the time of Frederick II's death in 1250 onwards, the power of the Empire became increasingly weak and the towns developed briskly. The principal business of the towns was long-distance trade. The Hanseatic League ports on the Baltic and North Sea coasts, especially Danzig, Lübeck and Hamburg, flourished. They were an important part of the 'Atlantic' seafaring community, who made significant technical advances in the design and rigging of ships capable of surviving in these seas, so much more challenging than the Mediterranean.[31] Other important towns grew up along the rivers, particularly the Rhine and the Danube and their tributaries, and on the roads connecting to the Alpine passes. These towns didn't attain the size of the great Italian centres. Cologne was probably the largest with about 30,000 citizens in the late 15th century. Nuremberg was next, while Augsburg and perhaps ten others may have had 20,000 people each.

Dealing in metals formed an important part of the trade in most fifteenth-century towns.[32] Only in the Low Countries did towns in the Empire get the large manufacturing industries that were common in Italy. Perhaps because they were not so populous and rich as Italian towns, their military strength did not attract noblemen to link their estates to the towns, thus making them into city states.[33] Eighty towns obtained substantial political independence as Free Imperial Cities. Each city was normally dominated by its rich merchants who controlled all the political levers. This probably reflected the distribution of wealth. A tax return for Augsburg in 1475 shows wealth concentrated as in Florence in 1427, rather than spread more widely as in Orvieto in 1292.

---

[31] Landstrom, 1961, pp 70-3, 76-7, & 90-7.
[32] For example, Scott, 1986, p 51.
[33] Scott, 2001, p 212.

Table 5 Augsburg 1475 Tax Return

Number of households	% of total	cum %	Tax paid (gulden)	% of total	cum %
52	1.2%		1,860	32.0%	
74	1.7%	2.9	1,240	21.3%	53.3
423	9.8%	12.7	1,976	34.0%	87
952	22.1%	34.8	742	12.7%	100
2,807	65.2%	100	none		
Totals 4,308	100.0%		5,818	100.0%	

Source: Paas, 1979, p. 64.

As in Italy fustian manufacture settled in a major linen-producing area - the Danube basin. But the organization of the industry was different in Germany from that in Italy, probably due to the wealth of the towns' merchant elites. In Germany the towns, rather than the guilds, ensured quality. They inspected the raw cotton and then stamped their seal on the finished cloth. The merchants were free to organize the spinning and weaving, not only in their own town, but wherever in the countryside or other towns they could recruit labour. The Swabian industry concentrated on the cheaper grades, which were usually sold either bleached white or dyed black. They did not compete with the high-quality, coloured fabric produced in Italy but they built up a great volume of production. Over 100,000 cloths per year were sealed in Ulm around 1500. In Memmingen the 124 weavers of 1420 had doubled to 256 by 1530 and totalled 403 in 1625. In 1601 more than 7 million yards of fustian was sealed in Augsburg alone.[34]

In Germany, as in the rest of northern Europe, the 14th century saw the break-up of many of the rigidities of serfdom. The terrible famines of the decade 1310-20 were followed by the Black Death in 1349. The population fell dramatically. Farms were left untilled and villages deserted. Country people moved to the towns where they earned higher wages and became free men. For example,

---

[34] Mazzaoui, 1981, pp 138-44, Sreenivason, 2004, p 267.

Hans Fugger, a weaver, moved to Augsburg from the village of Graben in 1367. Others stayed in the country but became free citizens of towns (*Ausburghers*). Many more old serfs moved onto the farms of other lords, where they paid less rent. Wages rose strongly and rents fell so that landlords' incomes declined and some became heavily indebted. The earnings of working families rose and some began to acquire a little capital, as their payments to landowners diminished. Many seemed to enjoy a golden age as they thought their medieval shackles had gone for good. New products appeared. For example it is thought that the first European-made needles were produced in Nuremberg in the 14th century.[35] It was probably in the 15th century that German towns were economically most vigorous. Around 1450 John Gutenberg in Mainz developed moveable metal type for printing, and at the same period merchants in the Tyrol opened up the copper and silver mines which were to enrich the Fugger family so greatly. Many of the former serfs were working in their own little businesses both in the towns and the country. The largest groups were in textile-manufacture and metal-working, but others were tending vineyards and growing dyers' plants in the country, or working at crafts like shoe and harness-making in the towns. The culture of these small businessmen favoured equality and economic freedom.

South Germany in the 15th century might have begun to develop as Holland and England did in the 16th and 17th centuries. The last vestiges of serfdom could have melted away, country people might have acquired some rights in the land they occupied, and a free peasantry and free burghers could together have developed a commercial, innovative economy. There seem to have been two main reasons why this did not happen. First, there was no strong central government able to bring law to the whole Empire. This encouraged the princes and their local nobles to carve out their own jurisdictions with much violence and feuding.[36] Secondly, landowners and their rapacious mortgagee/leaseholders decided to repair their finances by reimposing serfdom. The impositions of every kind that this policy inflicted on the tenants led to many local

---

[35] Jones, 1978, p 355.
[36] Zmora, 1997, pp 42-62.

rebellions (*Bundschuhs*), for example at Hegau in 1460, Selestat in 1493, Speyer in 1502, and Breisgau in 1513.[37] The independent and innovative culture of the small businessmen had also given rise to new religious ideas which presented further challenges to the old aristocracy. Preachers of all kinds had multiplied, among whom Luther and Zwingli are now the most famous. Scott and Scribner tell us that 'The leading role of evangelical preachers in bringing on the Peasants' War of 1525 is now indisputable.'[38] The insurgents temporarily gained control of more than a third of Germany. This appalling calamity for the landowners confirmed them in the view that they must tighten their control over 'the subject population'.

To illustrate how these events affected cotton manufacture I take some examples from a recent study of the estates of the Monastery of Ottobeuren, about 35,000 hectares adjoining the city of Memmingen, whose tenants were mostly engaged in spinning cotton and making linen warps. The Abbey was so impoverished by 1400 that a large number of farms were sold to tenants on a heritable tenure (*Erblehenrecht*), by which the rent was fixed in perpetuity. These were new farms made by clearing woodland in upland areas.[39] The principal old farms on the best lowland arable land continued to be let to serfs – or tenants who agreed to become serfs – on rents fixed in grain not in money. After the occupation of the monastery by the peasants in the War of 1525, the Abbey worked hard to reimpose serfdom. For example, in 33 hamlets in Ottobeuren parish, the percentage of serfs in the total population increased from 35.2% in 1564 to 93.5 % in 1627-8. The monks instituted new taxes and controls and created a bureaucracy to enforce them. In Ottobeuren serf rolls were drawn up listing all the inhabitants – men, women and children. The number of marriage fees and death duties collected annually increased from 4 and 7 in 1527-8 to 15 and 73 in 1586-9. A new excise tax on wine was begun in 1564 and annual property taxes came into existence by 1603. Inventories of all the wealth of every tenant were made

---

[37]Scott, 2002, pp 279-80; Blickle, 1981, p xiii.
[38] Scott & Scribner,1991, p 3.
[39] Sreenivasan, 2004, pp 16 – 21.

every three or four years from 1621 onwards, so that the net wealth of every peasant could be taxed appropriately.[40]   These measures led to a massive increase in the annual income of the Ottobeuren Monastery.   From 2,864 gulden in 1527/8 and 3,887 in 1528/9, it rose to 40,493 gulden in 1619/20.[41]   It was this great wealth which later enabled the monastery to build its marvellous flamboyant new church between 1748 and 1766.   At the same time as the monastery was growing rich it sought to strengthen its political position in the country, by favouring the leading peasant families, who typically formed an oligarchy monopolizing the positions of authority in the villages.   The distribution of wealth became less equal, as is shown in Fig. 1 below.   There was a similar change in the distribution of wealth in the Langenburg district of the County of Hohenlohe.[42]

Fig. 1   The distribution of wealth in nine Ottobeuren villages, 1525 and 1620.[43]

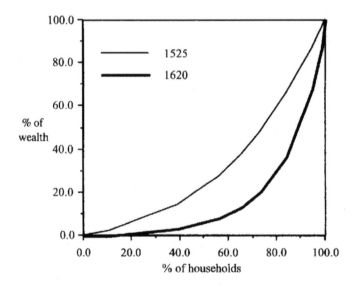

In 1601, in another effort to increase the monastery's wealth, the Abbot persuaded the Emperor to confirm his old (but disused)

[40] Sreenivason, 2004, pp 139-44.
[41] Sreenivason, 2004, p 138.
[42] Robisheaux, 1989, pp 84-5, 264-5.
[43] Sreenivason, 2004, p 146,

rights to force the tenants to make all their sales in the Ottobeuren market. This greatly increased the toll income of the market at the expense of the tenants, who now had to cart their produce up to 10km to Ottobeuren where they might get a worse price than they could have got half a kilometre from home. It also brought conflict with Memmingen whose '*Bannmeile*' (to protect **their** market tolls) extended 7kms into the Ottobeuren lands. The resulting increase in smuggling and fines probably damaged the competitive position of local fustians so much that the export trade was already lost before the whole area was completely devastated by the Swedish and Imperial armies in the 1630s.[44] In other areas of South Germany the urban oligarchies and the landed princes – the two groups with most of the wealth – cooperated better. The Dukes of Wurtemberg and fourteen merchant families in the Calw area colluded to keep the local worsted industry in stunted poverty for two centuries.[45]

4   European wealth creation reviewed, 1500 and 1600

Having brought the story of Italy and Germany to 1600 it is appropriate to return to Maddison's figures in Table 1. He shows Italy in about 1500 as the richest country in Europe with GDP per capita of $1,100 (International Dollars 1990 value). This figure had more than doubled since 1000 AD and we have seen some of the main reasons for this. After Italy, in 1500, came Belgium with a *per capita* GDP of $875. Belgium owed its position to being the centre of the great developments in woollen textile production in this period. The rest of the West European nations were close to the average of $771. This is an amazing 80% more than the figures for 1000 AD. What had happened?

Firstly, perhaps, were the developments in agriculture across the whole of northern Europe. The introduction of the heavy plough, drawn at first by oxen and then later by horses, was very significant. There were continuous improvements in arrangements for harnessing these animals, at first with wood and hemp, then with leather, and eventually incorporating the whipple tree to link the animals to the plough. This allowed much more land to be

---

[44] Sreenivason, 2004, pp 266-74.
[45] Ogilvie, 1997.

cleared and cultivated. Three-field systems allowed for crop rotation which reduced the need for fallow. More grazing land meant more animals could be reared and so there was more manure for the arable land. Other technical developments were water-mills for corn and later, in wool-producing areas, for fulling. A few windmills were built on flat, open sites. The greater range of textiles that we have already described and the much improved shipping and financial systems greatly encouraged trading, which in turn permitted more specialization.

These were the ways the greater wealth was created but why did it happen between 1000 and 1500, and why in Europe? We have seen that the Romans and the Abbasid Caliphate both made increases in *per capita* GDP for a period, but neither was able to sustain their growth. Since the 19th century, the word 'feudal' has been seen as a term of abuse in English politics and history, but could the feudal system of government in Europe have been beneficial to economic development? Although feudal medieval government was in the hands of a small number of barons and lords of manors, assisted by bishops and rectors, the kings were not quite like oriental potentates. Their estates were big but not large enough for them to be able to build really large palaces, and they could raise an army only with the willing consent of the lords of manors. This led to a consenual element in government. Discussions were held in the king's courts, which came to be called Parliaments, where land-owners, bishops and business leaders discussed making war and providing the taxes to pay for it. Separate king's courts were created where justices made laws to try to prevent the barons fighting with each other. At the village level the existence of manor courts, with their juries and township (or parish) meetings, may have been important by involving almost all heads of households in some decision making.

Lords of manors owned their lands – at least by the end of the 12th century. They profited directly from the growing output on their demesne lands and probably were able to extract more rent from their more prosperous tenants. They were willing to invest in water mills to improve the wealth of their tenants. They invested in iron production so that they could make cannon for their wars. They had some flexibility in managing their lands. In the North-West of England, instead of the three-field system used on flat Midland land, the Lords of old Cheshire manors, in the Arley area, created five to ten common fields in the sloping lands of Sutton Weaver and Great Budworth. In the 12th century they ceased making common fields and allocated fields adjoining the house to each farm.

Unfortunately Maddison did not produce wealth figures for the centuries between 1000 and 1500. Until the Black Death in 1350 the general tendency was for the population, food prices and rents all to rise, so it seems likely that the lords got the greater share of the new surplus wealth if there was more than enough to supply the growing population. But after 1350 food prices and rents fell because of the smaller population and wages rose strongly, so that wealth became more evenly distributed. Exactly how this worked out depended on the legal system of land tenure in each country. We have seen how, in Florence, many of the rural population became poor share-croppers; in Germany and England workers took farms at low rents and became richer; in the Netherlands many farmers acquired freehold land. The reason for the huge rise in Maddison's figures[46] for W. European *per capita* wealth is that the GDP of the area rose from \$10.9bn in 1000 AD to \$44.2bn in 1500. During that period the population only just over doubled from 26 million to 57 million. What he does not discuss is what the population was before the famines of 1310-20 and the Plague of 1349. If the population had been closer to 100 million at one time, the rise in wealth *per capita* should be attributed to the disaster rather than to the style of Government. Certainly the disasters were an important element in the wealth redistribution in several countries. The large area of land that had been put into cultivation and the many improvements in technology and trade were of course largely unaffected by the population decline, so the wealth of the area was much less affected than its population. Famine and disease may have been major causes of West Europe's increase in wealth. After 1500 the Low Countries steamed ahead. Antwerp became the great market for the pepper and spices brought back

---

[46] Maddison, 2007, Table 2.1, p 70.

from Indonesia by the Portuguese and the gold and silver obtained by the Spaniards in Mexico and Peru. Improvements in Dutch shipping enabled them to import their grain needs from the Baltic and concentrate on the dairy farming that they could do best. Their manufactures, their trading and their ships made them the most advanced commercial and industrial economy in Europe.

As we have seen, the North Italian cities had turned away from entrepreneurial endeavour in the 15th century as wealth became concentrated in fewer lands. The attraction of the artistic beauties of the Renaissance in architecture, in painting and in literature triumphed over the challenges of business. They failed to improve their ships so that they could compete with the more robust and superior models developed by nations with an Atlantic coastline. It was the Portuguese who sailed round the Cape of Good Hope and it was Ferdinand of Aragon who financed Columbus (born in Genoa) to sail across the Atlantic and discover America. The North German cities of the Hanseatic League were also virtually unrepresented in Atlantic travel. Having been much involved with the improvement of ships between 1300 and 1500, these cities were mostly confined within their walls by the aggressive princes after 1525. With their hinterlands in a different jurisdiction they did not flourish. Wealth *per capita* in Italy between 1500 and 1600 did not grow at all and in Germany it increased only from $688 to $791.

By contrast, between 1500 and 1600 the *per capita* wealth of the Netherlands grew by 81% from $761 to $1,381. It replaced Italy as the richest country in Europe. Like Italy in the 12th and 13th centuries, much land was in the hands of freehold farmers who became rich as a result of the rise in land values. Colonies of merchants and a shipping and ship-building industry grew up in the midst of these farm populations. The rule of law was established in all areas but there was no King and government was decentralized to the towns and provinces, also in the manner of the North Italian towns. A vigorous business culture developed and was allied with Lutheran and Calvinist reformed religion. Neighbouring Belgium was quite different. An autocratic Hapsburg government, with a passion for enforcing the old religion, reduced wealth growth to only 11% (from $875 - $976). The French, also, retained their old government and religion but wealth in France had been significantly increased in the mostly upland areas where the new religion had developed and a wider distribution of wealth had occurred. As a result, overall wealth had increased 15% which was close to the average for West European countries. UK wealth had increased from $714 to $974 - a growth of 36% - the second best in Europe. In the next section we will see why.

5   Lancashire 1600 – 1700

In the 15th and 16th centuries the best grades of cotton were shipped from the eastern Mediterranean in large, lightly armed sailing ships, mostly to Genoa and Venice, from whence it was distributed. Before the last quarter of the 16th century English ships were rare visitors to the Mediterranean. By this time French, Dutch and English ships incorporated the much improved technology developed on the Atlantic coast. With their large crews and numerous guns they were more than a match for the 'Barbary pirates' who came to frequent North African ports at this period and did so much damage to the slow, poorly armed Italian ships.[47] The failure of Italian and South German merchants to keep up with the new shipping technology is an indication of their entrepreneurial weakness.

 In 1581, a group of London merchants were granted a charter to trade with Turkey. Twenty-seven voyages were made before 1592 when a new Charter, with a bigger group of 53 merchants, was granted.[48] The London merchants' main interest in trading with the Levant was to obtain silks and dried fruits, like currants and sultanas, while cotton was third in importance. Nevertheless, by 1600 this new Levant Company was bringing in large quantities of raw cotton in most years for which records survive.[49] In this way the market for bulk cotton was transferred to London and Amsterdam, while the Germans and the Italians had greater difficulty in securing supplies at attractive prices. This hastened

---

[47] Davis, 1961, pp 126 - 9.
[48] Wood, 1933, pp 11-20; Davis, 1961, pp 126 – 31.
[49] Willan, 1955, p 408; Millard, 1956.

the decline of their industries.[50] This was the background to the first regular arrival in London of cotton fibre in bulk, direct from the Levant.

By 1600 fustians from Italy and Germany were well known in England. For example, in a small Cheshire village the shop-keeper had 'Osborne' (Augsburg) and 'Millan' (Milan) fustians for sale in 1612.[51] The arrival of raw cotton direct from the Levant allowed fustians to be made in England more cheaply than they could be imported. Where would they be manufactured? There were three main reasons why the industry settled in East Lancashire. First it was an area with ample supplies of linen yarn of its own production as well as, since 1535, additional supplies, as needed, from Ireland.[52] Secondly, between 1500 and 1650 the hill country in the east of the county, scarcely inhabited earlier, enjoyed a substantial immigration of new settlers, providing cotton spinners. Lastly, there was, as we shall see, a good supply of active small capitalists to organize production.

---

[50] Mazzaoui, 1981, p 54.
[51] Cheshire Record Office Inventory of R. Dewsbury of Gt Budworth.
[52] Lowe, 1972, p 12.

Map 1   The woollen and linen areas in Lancashire in 1600

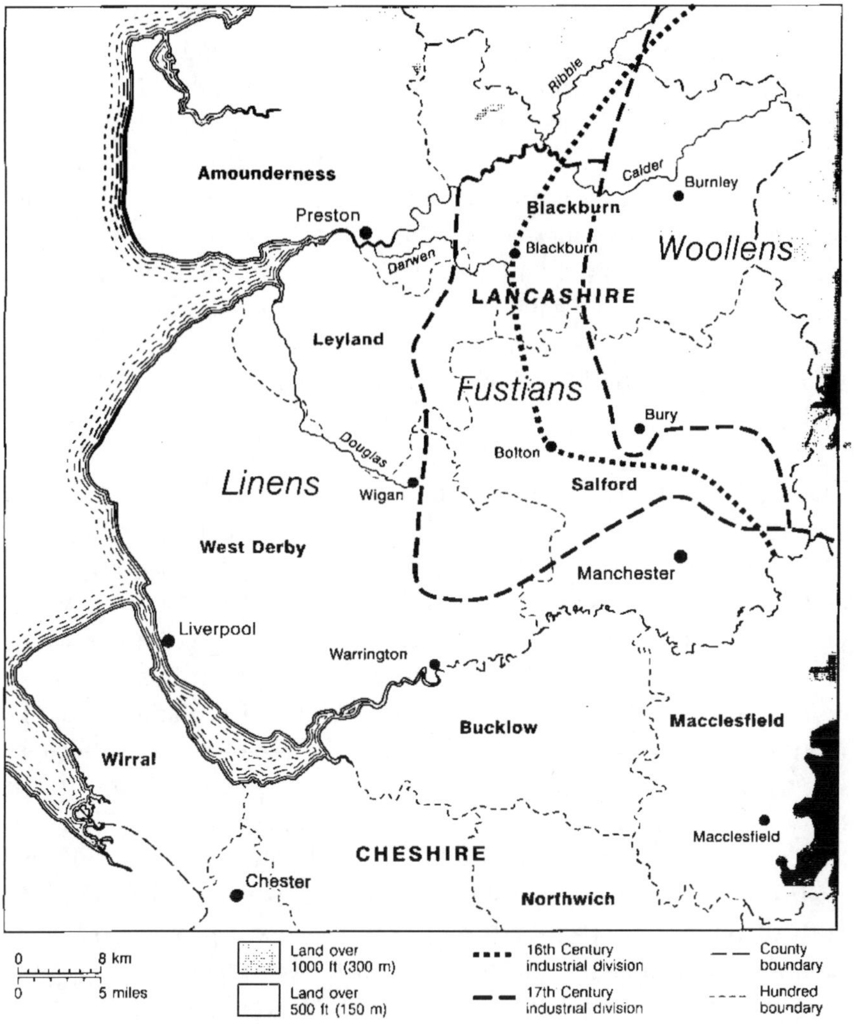

Labels on map:

Ribble

Amounderness

Calder

Burnley

Preston

Blackburn

Blackburn

Darwen

Woollens

LANCASHIRE

Leyland

Fustians

Bury

Douglas

Bolton

Linens

Wigan

Salford

West Derby

Manchester

Liverpool

Warrington

Bucklow

Macclesfield

Wirral

Macclesfield

CHESHIRE

Chester

Northwich

Legend:

0 — 8 km	Land over 1000 ft (300 m)	•••• 16th Century industrial division	— — County boundary
0 — 5 miles	Land over 500 ft (150 m)	— — 17th Century industrial division	- - - Hundred boundary

Source: Wadsworth & Mann, Cotton Trade, *pp. 24 & 79.*

Map 1 shows the 16th century division between the woollen and the linen areas. Fustian production settled into this borderland and was divided fairly equally between the Blackburn and Salford Hundreds.

Fustian manufacture, probably mostly of 'jeans' and denims but also of some dense cloths for covering pillows and mattresses and for making pockets, appears to have started in the Bolton-Manchester area around 1600. From the surviving references to nine people engaged in the trade between 1601 and 1612 it would appear likely that the spinning and weaving were probably done to the north in the Bolton area and the dyeing and marketing around Manchester - already a major commercial textile centre with a lot of experience in dyeing and finishing woollens. Fustian cutting - the making of 'tufts' (which created a fabric probably similar to corduroy) - seems to have been a speciality of the Blackley area between the two.[53] The trade quickly spread further north to the Blackburn area where there were at least 10 people engaged in it by 1609.[54]

The best information about the changing social and economic structure in the fustian areas is provided by an analysis of two sets of tax returns. Those of the 1543-5 Lay Subsidy for the early years and the 1660 Poll Tax and the 1664 Hearth Tax for later years. Only three complete returns of the 1660 Tax survive in the whole country. One is for Blackburn Hundred, for which there is also a 1543 return, so these will be the main focus of the analysis. The North-West of England was different to the South and East because it was dominated by pastoral rather than arable farming. In the early 16th century almost all its population lived on small farms averaging around 25 acres. Each household normally grew enough grain for its own use and lived on that and its animal produce. Its cash income came from selling cattle and textiles made from the hemp, wool or flax also grown on almost every farm.

The tax returns show that between the 1540s and the 1660s there came into existence a new group of small capitalists. The first reason for this unusual development was a change in property law in the late 15th century, which gave rights to the occupiers of farmland as customary tenants or copyholders. The second reason was that the market value of lowland land in Lancashire and

---

[53] D. Winterbottom's chapter in Roberts, 1998, pp 32-4.
[54] Wadsworth and Mann, 1931, pp 36-7

Cheshire rose strongly from a rent of around 7d or 8d an acre in 1540 to about 11s an acre in 1660. These two changes made most farming families the owners of valuable property which many increased by business or farming activities.[55] The Blackburn and Salford Hundreds, in which cotton manufacture became established, included much upland country which had been only very lightly populated in the medieval period. Some of the differences can be seen in Table 6, which compares the 1543-5 Tax return of Blackburn with that of the Bucklow Hundred in North Cheshire,[56] although both returns are incomplete. Blackburn lists taxpayers who paid £100-10-4 out of the total of £123-19-10 actually collected. One or two membranes of the return are missing and there is damage to the survivors. Many sheets continue the previous township without a heading and it is uncertain whether the present order of sheets is correct. The Shireburn and Townley families are missing and they were probably the largest landowners. Nevertheless what survives probably provides a sound view of the general position. Much more detail on the Bucklow return and the general propositions in this paragraph are given in my *Capital and Innovation* (2004), pp. 44-98. The 1543-5 tax returns for the North of England are much more comprehensive than the 1524 returns.[57]

[55] Foster, 2004, pp. 46-67; Allen, 1988, p 43; Allen, 1992, pp 55-77.
[56] The National Archive E179/130/125. Bucklow, Cheshire Record Office. DLT/F64.
[57] Swain, 1986, p 106, note 136 & Tait, 1924, pp 1 – 57.

Table 6 Blackburn and Bucklow Hundreds 1543-5

Blackburn Hundred, Lancashire (upland), contrasted with
Bucklow Hundred, Cheshire (lowland)

	Blackburn				Bucklow			
	No	%	Tax paid £ - s - d	% of tax	No	%	Tax paid £ - s - d	% of tax
Well-off families								
Taxed on Lands: Assessed at more than £10 p.a.	9	0.5	11- 11 - 4	11.5	25	1.5	47 -12- 3	53.5
Assessed at £5-£10 p.a.	21	1.2	4 - 10 - 0	4.5	24	1.5	2- 13- 11	3
Taxed on Goods: assessed at £10 or more	87	5	47- 7- 4	47.1	58	3.5	13 -12- 4	15.3
Total well-off families	117	6.7	63 - 8 - 8	63.1	107	6.5	63 -18- 6	71.8
Ordinary families								
Taxed on lands valued at £1-£4 p.a.	53	3	2-3-8	2.1	28	1.7	12-3	0.6
Taxed on goods valued at £1-£9	1585	90.3	34-19-0	34.7	1513	91.8	24-9-3	27.6
Total ordinary families	1638	93.3	37-1-8	36.8	1541	93.5	25-1-6	28.2
Grand totals	1757	100	100-10-4	100	1648	100	89-0-0	100

The rates of tax in the 1543-5 Subsidy were sharply raked with the rich landed gentry paying 5% and the poor farmers paying only 0.5%. This no doubt reflected the ability to pay and it means that the amount of tax paid is the best indication of the wealth of each group. The assessments are probably about one third of the real values.[58]

The first thing to notice in Table 6 is the modest position of the landed gentry in Blackburn. In Bucklow 25 families paid 53.5% of the total tax paid by the Hundred, whereas in Blackburn there were only 9 such families paying just 11.5% of the total. The reason for this was that in the Blackburn Hundred old gentry estates existed only in the valleys of the Ribble, Calder and Darwen rivers, where there was sufficient flat land under 63m (200ft) above sea level for barley and oats to be grown on demesne and tenanted land. The higher lands in Blackburn were hardly occupied in the Middle Ages. Around 1507 the main landowner, the Duchy of Lancaster (the Crown), had created many new copy-holds there. These copy-holders and a few freeholders had, by the 1540s, organized a new type of farming which made the second big difference with Bucklow.[59] In that Cheshire Hundred, the 58 families paying tax on their goods assessed at £10 or more consisted mostly of businessmen in Knutsford and Altrincham and lawyers and monks at Halton and Norton. In Blackburn the 87 families in this category were mostly people owning herds of cattle and sheep that fed on the grass on the higher lands. Some of them were also clothiers who organized woollen cloth manufacture.[60]

Extending from the main broad river valleys were many streams coming down from narrower defiles in the hills. Small settlements of a few houses with gardens and little fields occupied the lands beside the streams and the hills rose unfenced to the open moors at the top. The 'old' rents of this upland were very low, usually about 2½d per statute acre, and the market value in the 1540s was probably not more than 4d an acre. Only the enclosed lands paid rent, the right to graze animals on the hills being attached by custom to each enclosed acre. So land on which a herd of cattle lived might have a rental value of only £1 - £2 *per annum,* whereas

---

[58] Foster, 2004, pp 48 & 54.

[59] Tupling, 1927, p 235.

[60] Lancs. Record Office. My analysis of inventories from the 1570s and 1580s of testators with the same surnames as the 87 families.

the cattle might be worth £20 or £30. This was why these families were assessed on the value of their goods and not their lands. So the broad picture in the 1540s was that in both these Hundreds about 6.5% of households had about two thirds of the wealth and the other 93.5% had very little. In Bucklow the wealth was mostly in the hands of the landed gentry. In Blackburn it was different; most of the money belonged to commercial farmers although some of them had relations among the landed gentry.

By the 1660s a large new group of small capital owners had come into existence. The Poll Tax of 1660 was the most comprehensive national tax levied between the 1540s and the Land Tax of the 18th century. It was charged on three separate groups of people:

1) the major gentry (together with doctors and lawyers) paid fixed sums, ranging from £10 for esquires to £100 for dukes.
2) those whose income exceeded £5 p.a. paid 2% of it.
3) married couples and single men and women over 16 each paid one shilling.

One of the other two surviving returns of this tax is from the Northwich Hundred of Cheshire. From some very detailed archives of townships there I was able to establish that the assessments in (2) above were made on income from property, trading stock or money lent at interest, and that these assessments were pretty conservative, being often half or less than half of the income actually received.[61]

In Blackburn Hundred in 1660 25 people paid the fixed sums – one baronet, fifteen esquires, three widows and six attorneys. Together they paid £218, or 23% of the £946-3-2 raised by the tax. There were 1,343 assessments of £5 p.a. or more which raised £358 or 37.8% of the total. The Hearth Tax of 1664 recorded 4,596 households of whom 2,961 paid tax and 1,635 were exempt. Some families were assessed to Poll Tax on more than one property, for example a farm in one township and extra land in an adjoining township. Therefore it is reasonable to assume that there were only about 1,200 families with assessments of £5 or more. Putting these

---

[61] Foster, 2004, pp 144-9, 156-64.

figures together allows us to estimate the distribution of wealth in Blackburn as follows: -

Table 7 The Wealth of Blackburn Hundred
(estimated from the Poll Tax 1660[62] and the Hearth Tax 1664[63])

Number of Households	%	Social Group	Total Poll Tax paid by group	Likely income from capital per household	Likely capital assets of each household
			£	£ p.a.	£
25	0.5	Major Gentry, attorneys	218	150 - 3,000	3,000 - 60,000
1,200	26.1	Richer families	358	8 - 500	100 - 5,000
1,736	37.8	Medium families }		1 - 10	20 – 150
		}	371		
1,635	35.6	Poor families }		nil - 1	nil – 20
4,596	100		947		

Notes.
1. *4,596 is the total number of households assessed for Hearth Tax, from which 1,635 households were exempt.*
2. *Attorneys paid a fixed sum of £3, which assumed an income of £150 p.a.*
3. *The Poll Tax assessments for 'Richer families' were from £5 - £300 p.a. I have increased the figures for their likely incomes to take account of the conservative nature of the assessments.*

---

[62] The National Archive E179 250/4.
[63] The National Archive E179 86/145

In this table the 'Richer' families are those assessed on income of £5 *p.a.* or more in the Poll Tax. The 'Medium' families are those who were not so assessed but paid Hearth Tax. That tax[64] exempted households who occupied a house worth less than £1 *p.a.* and owned land and goods worth less than £10. Such people were poor, but not quite as poor as some historians have assumed. If it is assumed that these valuations were also conservative (which seems likely) one can estimate that some of them will have had assets worth up to £20 (nearly two years' annual earnings of a labourer). That there were quite a lot of people like this, on the borderline of exemption, is suggested by the fact that an additional 510 families paid Hearth Tax in Blackburn in 1667.

When we compare these 1660s figures with those of 1543-5, two things stand out. First, the population of Blackburn Hundred had approximately doubled. If we increase the figure of 1,755 households in Table 1 by 23%, to take account of the missing membranes, one can estimate that in the 1540s there were about 2,158 households compared to 4,596 in the 1660s. Other information confirms that the uplands on the eastern side of Lancashire and Cheshire all experienced great population growth in this period. C.B.Phillips compared[65] the figures for rural deaneries in 1563 with the Hearth Tax 1664 totals and found that the population of Macclesfield increased in that period by 222% , that of Manchester by 89% and Blackburn by 57%. This contrasts with small increases in the lowland areas, for example 19% in Frodsham (which included Bucklow Hundred) and only 14% in Leyland.

This difference between upland and lowland regions was connected with another distinction which assisted industrial development in the uplands. Lowland townships were usually owned by resident major gentry. In the North-West they had mostly put their tenants on three-life leases in the middle of the 16th century. These leases were somewhat less favourable to the tenants than copyholds, and

---

[64] 14 Chas II c 10.
[65] Phillips & Smith, 1994, p 9.

the tenants were not allowed to divide their land,[66] so there was no 'spare' land in these townships and only a few new cottages were built. In upland areas it was different. Much of the land was freehold or copyhold, held from the Crown or the Church. Manorial control was often far away and properties could be divided. In 1500 the population was low because it was difficult to grow grain above 200ft (63m). But with the development of markets in the 150 years leading up to 1660 it became possible for hill dwellers to be virtually certain that they could buy grain each year in the lowlands. New types of farming developed, like raising herds of cattle and sheep on the high pastures, and selling wool and animals to the growing populations in the South of England. Many of the hills contained coal which outcropped on the surface, providing a cheap supply of fuel. Coal mines were short-lived in this period, as they soon filled with water, so expensive drainage tunnels (adits) were required to allow mining to go deeper. Nevertheless a continuous supply of coal was achieved in many areas and this allowed industries like nail-making, lime-burning and brick-making to be established near the mines. As the population increased, quarrying for building stones and limestones for mortar created more employment. The transport of food into the hills and minerals out of them added to the activities available to the local popluation. All these jobs required fit young males and naturally they usually had wives and children. As spinning was usually done by women a large pool of new spinners was naturally created who could find work after 1600 helping to make the new fustians.[67]

Other social forces were also driving development in the hills. The well-off, three-life leaseholder in the lowlands had more than enough children to inherit the family farm. Younger sons were often apprenticed to an occupation and expected to fend for themselves. All children were usually given a portion, but if something went wrong - they either got no portion or lost it, or a

---

[66] Foster, 2004, pp 69-81.

[67] For the range of jobs and services available in the Bolton area in the 1580s and 1590s see Foster, 2002, pp 41-53. For North-East Lancashire 1500 – 1640, see Swain, 1986, especially ch. 7 & 8.

daughter fell in love with an unapproved man and so forfeited her portion - where could they go? Into the towns perhaps but they were expensive, unhealthy, and might not provide a job. Or they could go into the hills where they might put up a cabin to live in. Clitheroe Court Rolls record fines for 'encroachments' which often meant that the landlord was belatedly starting to charge rent on a piece of waste land on which a dwelling had been erected without his knowledge.[68] Another potent source of population growth was the subdivision of the copyholds. G.H.Tupling has analysed these subdivisions in 23 areas of Rossendale. In 1507 seventy-two copyholds were created; these had become 101 by 1527, 200 by 1608, and 314 by 1662. [69]

Another trend which stands out when comparing the 1540s and the 1660s in Blackburn is the appearance of the large social groups in between the major gentry and the poor. In 1545 the group immediately below the major gentry had numbered only 87 families. By 1660 the similar group were about 1,200 strong and they were worth, on average, £400 - £500 each. This group paid a total tax of £358 which was 2% of their assessed income. So the total income of the group was £17,900. If this was a yield of 5% on their capital, their total wealth was £358,000 or nearly £300 each. Allowing for the likelihood that the assessments were conservative they probably owned an average of £400 - £500 each.[70] As we have seen the main reason for this was the rise in the value of the land (usually copy-hold) that they owned.

In the 1540s land in the upland areas of Blackburn was much less valuable than that in the lowland areas, but from then until the 1660s its value rose at least as strongly. The higher common lands were mostly allotted to individual copy-holders in the early 17th century so that by the 1660s each farmer had full control of his land. The copy-holders had mostly bought out the Crown's rights before the Civil War so the land was effectively freehold. The wealth distribution shown in Table 2 was probably typical of the

---

[68] Tupling, 1927, p 61.
[69] Tupling, 1927, p 235.
[70] Foster, 2004, pp 150-1, for similar calculations for Northwich Hundred.

North-West. In the only other Hundred Return to survive – that of Northwich [71] - the major gentry were slightly richer, paying 35.6% of the Poll Tax collected in the Hundred, compared with 23% in Blackburn. In Northwich the richer families constituted 32.9% of the total number of householders, compared with 26.1% in Blackburn. But Northwich had not experienced the great population growth of Blackburn, whose new migrants are almost all likely to have been people without much capital. It is likely that conditions in Blackburn were repeated in Salford Hundred to the south, except that Manchester was a much more important business town than anywhere else in the North-West. Chester, with 1,686 hearths in 1664 to Manchester's 1,067, was larger, but it was a centre of government, the Church, the Law and the gentry, but not business. [72]

We can see that this East Lancashire society of small capitalists was already a business society from the way it organized the manufacture of fustians. The first people into action were the merchants. Several families of Manchester merchants had representatives in London, whose job was to sell the woollen and linen cloth that the Manchester-based partners bought and sent down to them. Around 1600 one or more of these London partners bought some of the newly arrived packs of raw cotton (called cotton wool) and sent them up to Manchester, where the partners there found businessmen to organize the manufacture. These people bought the cotton wool on extended credit – usually 3-6 months. They also bought linen yarn for warp, sometimes produced by local people and sometimes imported from Ireland. They found and trained spinners and weavers and produced cloth. Sometimes they sold this cloth back to the Manchester merchants from whom they had bought the cotton wool (thus extinguishing their debt) and sometimes they sold it to other, usually Manchester-based, dyers and 'chapmen'. These people had knowledge of the markets, and of the types of finishing their customers would like, so they prepared and sold the cloth, either in Britain, or to merchants in London, Hull or Bristol, who then exported it. The

---

[71] Foster, 2004, p 150.
[72] Crosby, 2008, p 3.

most famous Manchester merchants were the brothers George and Humphrey Chetham. George lived in London and Humphrey in Manchester. They started with capital of only a few hundred pounds, but by 1619 had increased it to £10,000. Humphrey, who survived his brother but never married, donated a third of his wealth to found the famous library and school in Manchester that both bear his name. A surviving document shows that between June and December 1626 George sent 36½ packs of cotton up to Manchester. Each pack weighed about 240 lbs and sold for about £21 to one of the twelve different customers.[73]

By 1621 Lancashire was said to be making 40,000 pieces of fustian a year.[74] A picture of a substantial fustian maker is provided by the inventory of John Collier of Bolton who died in 1668.[75] In merchandize he had:

	£ s d
in linen yarn and warpes	62- 0- 0
in the spinners' and websters' hands	50-10- 0
in cotton wool	97-10- 0
in weft (cotton)	3- 0- 0
in jeanes, plaines and barmillions	53-12- 0
in debts owed to him by 5 named persons	89-10- 0
in money lent and odd debts	25-10- 0
in money in the house	56- 0- 0
Total	437-12- 0

Other inventories tell us that fustian products in the 17th century were 'little cheanes', 'diamonds', 'grey and dyed thicksetts', 'branched and dyed tufts', 'pillows', 'pinks', 'ribs' and 'grey and white jeans'. A finished length, known as an 'end', varied in price from around 8s to 25s. The raw cotton was usually the most expensive component of the cost, while spinning and weaving often

---

[73] Guscott, 2003, pp 287-91.
[74] Wadsworth & Mann, 1931, p 15.
[75] Lancashire Record Office. Wills are indexed by name and date of probate.

each cost about half the value of the cotton. Spun and prepared warps frequently cost less than the cotton wool. In the 17th century the price of cotton was usually between 8d and 12d a lb but as it came from so far away political events and wars caused wider fluctuations, so that the price could be anything between 4½d and 21d per lb.

The size of the businesses operated by fustian makers varied enormously. James Waddington of Mellor, near Blackburn, died in 1664 while still working and had only £15-10- 0 worth of cloth and materials at the time of his death, compared with John Collier's stock worth £266-12- 0 (see above). The people who marketed the fustians were usually known as 'chapmen' but they might also be makers like 'George Andrews, chapman', of Bolton who died in 1694. Chapmen were usually richer than makers. At his death Andrews had -

	£ s d
989 ends of fustian and 404 bundles of yarn in wool, weft and yarne in work folks' hands	900-15- 3
Good debts	184-13- 6
Bad debts	63-12- 6
Total	£1,149- 1- 3

This society of small capitalists developed a culture that was supportive of the businesses that so many of them were engaged in. The culture emphasized the importance of business and the view that a life spent in a successful business was worthy of respect and admiration. A feature of their culture was the division of inheritances more or less equally between all the children, male and female alike, which continually spread wealth more widely. They tended to find the traditional religion too hierarchic and authoritarian and eagerly embraced the new Puritan approach, which supported their ideas of equality and independence. This transition was particularly easy in Lancashire because there were only a very small number of huge parishes like Whalley and

Blackburn. As the population in the hills increased congregations built and maintained their own chapels and appointed to them ministers who supported their culture. In this way a vigorous Puritan spirit became strongly established in the business communities in Blackburn and Salford Hundreds. Bolton became known as the Geneva of the North and in the Civil War they were among the staunchest supporters of the Parliamentary cause.

In the 1670s and 1680s the textile trades of western Europe were transformed by the appearance of large quantities of cotton cloth brought by the Dutch, French, and English from India. These cloths, brilliantly coloured in a great array of new designs, were light, cool, washable, and so cheap that they quickly became widely fashionable.   This was the situation that led to the mechanization of cotton spinning that is the subject of Section 6.

6 The Mechanization of Cotton Spinning
The cotton plant originated in India and by the early centuries of the Christian era it was probably being grown and manufactured into cloth all over this huge area. After the Arab conquest of the southern Indus valley in the 8th century, the growing of cotton was extended to the Middle East and slowly spread all the way along the North Aftrican coast to Spain and down into West Africa. Probably at a similar period it reached South-East Asia. People in southern China started to grow cotton in the 13th century. By the 16th century it had ousted linen to become the principal Chinese textile and in the 16th century it also spread to Japan. As well as growing, spinning and weaving cloth in every grade from the strongest sail-cloth to gossamer-fine veils for grand ladies, the Indians used a great array of mordants, dyestuffs and resists to create a kaleidoscope of different colour effects. They had a large trade selling their cottons – particularly the more expensive ones – to the Middle East, SE Asia and China. When the Dutch, French and English started carrying these cottons to Europe after 1650 they were only making a small addition to India's existing large export trade.[76] This section describes the reaction of the European market to the arrival of Indian cottons and the growth of English printing

---

[76] Riello & Partharati, 2009.

on a linen/cotton mix using much of the Indian dyeing and printing technology. It then describes in some detail the development of spinning machinery by Hargreaves, Arkwright and Crompton, and attempts to assess why this revolutionary machinery was produced in a little corner of the huge global cotton-manufacturing world, which had started with such poor and incomplete technical skill in cotton-spinning. It finishes with a discussion of the social, technical and wealth characteristics of the three 'inventors'.

As Indian cottons, and particularly the printed or painted designs, became popular in Europe in the 1670s and 1680s they provoked a growing protest from the manufacturers of light-weight woollens which were the mainstay of traditional clothing. These manufacturers feared their market was being stolen. The other problem for governments was that few European products had found a market in India so this flood of cottons had to be paid for with gold and silver. Printed calicos, as these new cloths were called, after Calicut on the west coast of India, were therefore banned in France in 1686. In England the government proceeded more slowly. In 1701 the use of or wearing of cotton cloth which had been printed, striped or checked in India was prohibited. This was an attempt to limit the cost of imports by confining them to plain white cloth. More than twenty years earlier European dyers had gone to India and learnt some of their techniques so that they could print European designs on Indian calico. European printers therefore flourished even more. In England an Excise Duty was imposed in 1712 and doubled to 6d a yard in 1714 but even that failed to stem the flood of cotton. So in 1721 the use of or wearing of any cloth containing cotton, that was printed, striped or checked, was banned.[77]

Among the small number of exceptions to this prohibition were the fustians traditionally made in Lancashire. This legislation left the fustian makers in a curious position. There is some evidence that they had been making striped and checked cloths since about 1700 and also that some fustians had been printed. Apparently they continued these activities after 1721 but did not expand them too

---

[77] Wadsworth & Mann, 1931, pp 116 - 9 & 129 - 39.

aggressively, because it was not until 1735 that Norwich woollen manufacturers started to prosecute retailers. The Manchester manufacturers then petitioned Parliament and a new Act in 1736 made all their business legal.[78] From that year onwards their trade grew quickly.

Lancashire cotton manufacturers were still using linen for warp and the weft was provided by the soft, weak cotton that they had used in fustians. This was 10-20 count cotton (10 hanks, each 840 yards long, weighing a total of 1lb was called 10 count) which was what their spinners could spin. But they had learnt to make a much flatter cloth that was more suitable for printing than the old fustian thicksetts. Although the linen warp made their cloth less good for dyeing than the all-cotton Indian calico, the English printers had much improved their technology. The Europeans had made other changes. In India most 'prints' were actually painted on each cloth, but in Europe printing with wooden blocks (as used by book printers) was quickly adopted. Lancashire remained an area with a large number of small textile businesses. In the first directory of Manchester and Salford (1773) over 500 are listed. By 1750 Lancashire cotton manufacturing techniques seem to have been the best in Europe.

From the Indians' point of view the changes in the European states' laws on cottons were unimportant. The amount of Indian textiles bought by the East India Company does not appear to have been affected by the laws passed in England on wearing Indian cottons. The Company continued to sell Indian cloth to English merchants who then re-exported it to Africa. They also sold cloths to merchants from all the other European countries who did not themselves trade with India.[79] The total amount of cotton used in Europe was only a small percentage of Indian production. There were millions of cotton workers in India and only tens of thousands in Europe and the quality of Indian spinning was still far superior to that of the Europeans. In Europe spinners could not produce a thread strong enough to make the warp for any grade of cotton

---

[78] Wadsworth & Mann, 1931, p 140.
[79] Chaudhuri, 1978, pp 540 - 5.

cloth. Indians, on the other hand, could spin both warp and weft of 40, 60 and 80 count to make the finest, lightest cloth imaginable, called by the English 'Muslins'. The Indians felt that they were still the centre of the world's cotton manufacture and trade and Europe was just a small market far away. In 1750, to suggest that England would revolutionize world cotton manufacture within 40 years would have been considered ridiculous. But this view failed to recognize that the European populations were the largest and richest in the world not to enjoy cotton as their principal textile. India, China, the rest of Asia and the Middle East all appreciated cotton's many attractions. Was it not an anomaly that it was hardly available in Europe?

As cotton goods became increasingly popular in England in the forty years before 1721 there were many people who realized that all-cotton cloth could never be made in England at a price competitive with Indian cloth because Indian wages were a fraction of English – around £2 - £3 p.a. – and both countries' workers used similar hand-operated tools. The Europeans would have to have a better machine. There was talk of such a machine but none appeared. However, in the six years before 1721, the sale of 2 million yards a year of English-printed cotton cloth had clearly demonstrated that there was a strong public demand. So when Parliament amended the rules in 1736 and allowed English-made linen warp/cotton weft cloth to be printed and sold in England there were plenty of people who thought its manufacture would quickly grow. Two of the quickest off the mark were Lewis Paul and John Wyatt, who patented their machine for spinning cotton in 1738. Factories were established in London, Birmingham, Northampton and Leominster. The machinery did spin cotton but the quality was poor and breakdowns were frequent. The businesses all lost money and the investors lost tens of thousands of pounds.[80] Why was this experiment a failure?

Paul and Wyatt had correctly identified that there was plenty of demand for spun cotton. However, neither of them came from a centre of excellence in either mechanical engineering or in cotton

---

[80] Wadswoth & Mann, 1931, pp 411- 448.

manufacture. In a document written in 1736[81] they had correctly forecast that their machine might be opposed by people whose jobs it might destroy. For this reason, it would seem, neither the inventors nor any of their investors ever asked anyone with cotton-spinning knowledge and experience from Lancashire - the only cotton-spinning area - to help them. In addition, their lack of precision-engineering knowledge seems to have resulted in their machines having many inaccurately made parts that quickly wore out and broke when the machine was worked: 'small fragile parts proved extremely expensive to maintain in good working order'.[82] Lancashire clock and watch makers could have made better machines if they had been asked to do so, but the rich London and Birmingham investors apparently did not know of their existence.

The following table illustrates how right Paul and Wyatt were to forecast a growing demand for spun cotton.

Table 8 Raw cotton imported and retained in Britain

average per year

years	000s lbs	note
1740-45	1,595	
1746-51	2,695	
1752-56	3,385	
1757-63	2,245	Seven Years War
1764-69	4,269	
1770-74	3,553	
1775-80	6,038	
1781-85	approx. 12,800	

Source: Wadsworth & Mann, 1931, p 521.

Lancashire cotton manufacturing firms busily recruited spinners in the 1740s. An example can be seen in the Latham family who lived in Scarisbrick - a long way west of the main cotton area -

---

[81] Wadswoth & Mann, 1931, p 417.
[82] Fitton, 1989, p 13.

whose 7 daughters became cotton spinners at this time.[83]   By the early 1750s the annual demand for cotton yarn had increased by 1.5 million lbs. This meant that there was a demand for at least 10,000 more spinners than had existed in the early 1740s. To clean, card, rove and spin one pound of raw cotton took one woman about two days, so her annual output was about 150 lbs. Many women were only able to work part-time and many had other jobs spinning wool or flax. The need for a machine to do this work must have been obvious to many people living in the cotton-manufacturing area. We know that two men there - Lawrence Earnshaw, 'celebrated for his mechanical genius', and James Taylor, a clock-maker - both made machines in the 1753 – 55 period.[84]   Neither machine ever came into use due to the social problems attendant on its introduction.   Earnshaw abandoned his machine lest it 'take the bread from the mouths of the poor' and Taylor was forced to give up his efforts 'by the ill treatment he received'.

The Seven Years' War, 1757 – 63, removed some of the incentive to improve spinning methods because it interfered with the supply of cotton from the Caribbean Islands and disrupted markets. However by the last half of the 1760s the pressure on spinning was greater than ever before.[85]   More cotton was now available for spinning and there was also a great demand for spinners from the sail-cloth industry, which expanded rapidly in the Lancashire area in the 1750s and 1760s. Because salt was exported from Cheshire via Liverpool to the Baltic ports, such as Riga, where the flax for making sail-cloth came from, Liverpool merchants were leaders in this trade. About 50,000 part-time spinners were working on yarn for sail-cloth.[86]   Linen and wool were widely spun in Britain but the technology for spinning those fibres was different from that required for cotton spinning. There were perhaps 15,000 full-time cotton spinners at work during the War of 1757 - 63. In the period 1764 - 9, when the amount of cotton needing to be spun nearly doubled, some 15,000 more spinners were required. Perhaps 4,000

---

[83] Foster, 2002, pp 161 – 2.
[84] Wadsworth & Mann, 1931, pp 472-3.
[85] See also Baines, 1835, p 115 and Guest, 1823, p 12.
[86] Foster, 2004, pp 274 and 296-7.

- 5,000 women who had spun before 1757 were able to return to the trade, but that left a requirement to recruit and train about 9,000 new spinners. Cotton spinning paid around 6d - 7d per day (see discussion below of spun cotton prices, p 91) compared with a female agricultural wage of 5d per day, so there was an incentive for new recruits to join the trade. However it took at least 2 - 3 months for a girl, assisted by a teacher, to learn to produce 1lb of good quality yarn every two days. So there were clearly periods when weavers were waiting for yarn. It was this shortage of cotton yarn that resulted in the famous developments connected with the names of Hargreaves and Arkwright.

Why were the two machines, separately developed by these two men, successful and how did they survive the opposition of the Lancashire spinners? Each had a different history. Hargreaves, born in 1721, was a cotton-weaver who lived with his wife and eight children in Stanhill near Blackburn – the northern centre of the industry. His daughter wrote that her father made his machine in 1766 so as to spin enough yarn to keep his two sons weaving.[87] In 1767 he showed his machine to four manufacturers - Howarth, Peel, Hindle and Pollard - and two other men. He also made and sold machines to a number of people. However a mob burned Hargreaves' barn and the parts of twenty machines he was making. The next year, 1768, he took up an invitation to move to Nottingham to work as a partner of a Mr Shepley, evidently thinking that he could thereby avoid the anger of the spinners in Lancashire. He soon changed to become a partner of Mr James, and together they set up a factory full of his machines which came to be known as 'jennies'. Hargreaves managed this factory until 1777.[88] Nottingham was a good place to site the factory because of the existence there of the framework-knitting industry. This industry had originally made only silk stockings but started making knitted cotton stockings in the 1730s. As there were no spinners in the area they bought cotton yarn from Lancashire.

---

[87] Aspin, 1968, pp 119 - 121.
[88] Aspin, 1964, pp 23 - 5.

Hargreaves died in 1778. He was not a mechanical engineer but his knowledge of cotton-spinning enabled him to make a simple machine which worked to produce the same coarse, soft, weft yarn that hand-spinners produced. His machine was quickly improved upon by Lancashire people with greater mechanical knowledge. In October 1770 it was reported in the *Manchester Mercury* that 'there are several …sorts …of engines for drawing, spinning and twisting cotton' in use.[89] In June 1769 seven spinning machines in three different manufacturers' premises in the Bolton/Bury area were destroyed by rioters.[90] These were probably Hargreaves-type machines. A much improved version with 24 spindles was offered for sale and illustrated in the *Pennsylvania Magazine* in 1775.[91] The use of the jenny, with its 8, 16 or 24 spindles, transferred the production bottleneck from spinning to the preparatory processes of cleaning, carding and roving, and there is evidence that many improvements in the equipment carrying out these processes were tried out. The jenny did not at first make a large reduction in the cost of cotton yarn but it did allow larger quantities to be produced. By the 1820s, when the number of spindles on one machine had been increased to 120 and the preparatory machinery had also been improved, it was probably capable of producing low-count yarn as cheaply as any machine then in existence. In the early 1770s the practice that had emerged for the manufacturers to hand out raw cotton to the weavers may have helped to reduce hostility to mechanization.[92] This may, for example, have allowed a group of spinners working in the same hamlet as two or three weavers to 'share' a jenny between them to keep their weavers supplied. According to evidence to the House of Commons in 1780, manufacturers paid jenny-spinners up to 2s 6d per day.[93] The stability of demand at this time may also have assisted. For whatever reason no more machine-breaking is recorded before 1779.

---

[89] Aspin, 1964, p 48.
[90] Rose, 1963-4, p 67.
[91] Aspin, 1964, p 45.
[92] Ogden, 1783, 1968 ed., p 88.
[93] Journals of the House of Commons, vol 37, pp 925 - 6.

The history of the Arkwright machinery is much more dramatic because it changed European-made cotton cloth technology. Very little was known about it before the late R.S. Fitton's biography of Arkwright was produced in 1989.[94] He obtained access to the archives of the Smalley and Arkwright families and so was able to produce a much more detailed picture of events than earlier historians. This has allowed a much better understanding of the technical and economic forces at work. However Fitton's book makes little attempt to discuss the remaining gaps in the story, perhaps because he died before completing it. I have used my experience running a small tool-making business to fill in the major gaps. The passages that depend on my business and technical knowledge are in italics.

It has always been known that Richard Arkwright was born in 1732 and became a peruke-maker and barber in Bolton, a cotton manufacturing centre. He realized that a successful spinning machine would make someone a fortune. In 1767 he employed John Kay, a clock-maker in Warrington, to make a model of an abandoned design of Thomas Highs. Highs was a skilled and knowledgeable tool-maker who had previously employed Kay on this project. Kay's model was taken to Preston, where Arkwright's family roots were, and Kay worked on the machine which was disguised as one to 'find longitude'.[95] In Preston, Arkwright recruited two distant relations, John Smalley and David Thornley, and they all went to Nottingham where, in May 1768, they made an agreement to become equal partners in the business of constructing spinning machinery. With Thornley was his brother-in-law, Henry Brown, a watch-maker. In June 1768 a patent was applied for, in Arkwright's name, which was granted in July 1769. On 29 September 1769 they agreed to rent a site in Nottingham to build a factory. In the seventeen months between their arrival in Nottingham and this agreement[96] it is to be supposed that the two technically qualified employees, Kay and Brown, were busy

---

[94] Fitton, 1989.

[95] The Admiralty was offering a large prize to the inventor of a machine which would find longitude.

[96] Fitton, 1989, p 26.

experimenting with the spinning machine which had been made in Preston. No doubt they will have improved it and evolved designs for the cleaning, carding and roving machines that would be required to feed the spinning machines. It seems likely that Smalley had returned to Preston and stayed mostly there where he had a family. Arkwright and Thornley were probably occupied in supplying materials for the new machinery, obtaining labour to assist their 'engineers', and raw cotton for them to work with. Most importantly, because the three partners did not have the necessary capital, they were looking for financial backers to help them build a factory on the site in Nottingham. In January 1770 two other men joined the team. Samuel Need and Jedediah Strutt became co-partners with the other three on payment of £500 between them. *This suggests that the three original partners had by this stage invested some £500 - £600 in the business so that with the new £500 the five partners had around £1,000 - £1,200 invested. It was probably part of the agreement that Need and Strutt would lend the business money at 5% or other reasonable interest rate to finance the building work, the cost of making all the machinery and the start-up costs of getting the factory into production.* Arkwright and Thornley were to be paid £25 each per annum to provide day-by-day management.

The machine developed at this time, although it later acquired the name of a 'Water-frame', was initially powered by horses. We do not know much about this factory. Aspin suggests it was slightly smaller than 150ft x 30ft[97]. It seems that its wheel-house was 30ft in diameter and 11ft high and designed for 6 or 9 horses to keep the wheel in motion.[98] In 1772 there were estimated to be 300 people employed there.[99] So it seems likely that it was similar in size to the first Cromford mill (described below) which also employed 300 people in the 1770s. Need and Strutt were both capable businessmen who had started work as apprentices and by this stage had spent many years in the framework-knitting world making hosiery. Need was more of a marketing expert, while Strutt was a

---

[97] Aspin, 1964, p 36.
[98] Fitton, 1989, p 66.
[99] Aspin, 1964, p 37.

fully qualified technical manager, in whom Need had complete confidence. It seems likely that Strutt, as the man disbursing the money for building and equipping the new factory, and as the most qualified technician, would have become the technical leader of the team. The fact that the machinery produced a thread that was ideal for hosiery indicated that a knowledge of that technology had been important at an early stage: the Lancashire group is unlikely to have had this knowledge. The Nottingham factory was probably, from the beginning, equipped with the doubling and reeling machinery to process further the basic cotton yarn to make it suitable for hosiery. This machinery is described in the survey of the Robinsons' mill at Papplewick in 1784.[100] *This new factory was probably producing and selling yarn to the hosiers by the end of 1770. They must have had sufficient orders by mid-1771 to ensure that the Nottingham factory would be in full production in 1772. It also seems that they had market information suggesting that, if they could produce it, they would be able to sell twice as much yarn. In August 1771 they decided to build a factory powered by a water mill at Cromford in the Derbyshire Peak district.*[101] This was a five-storey factory and it would seem that it too received more orders than expected because they ran a night shift for many years. This was evidently necessary because the water supply was insufficient to run all the machinery simultaneously.

The reason for the increase in orders for this business may have been that by the end of 1773 they had extended their market from the hosiers into the supply of yarn for plain cotton cloth for printing.[102]. This happened because it turned out that their yarn was also ideal for using as warp for this cloth. This was one part of the revolution brought about by the 'water-frame', as this spinning machine came to be called. The other was that the machinery could spin yarn which was much finer than the yarn normally produced by hand-spinners. We know, from the stock-book records of a Blackburn firm called Cardwell, Birley and Hornby,

---

[100] Notts. Record Office, DD 4P 79/63.
[101] Fitton, 1989, p 28.
[102] Fitton, 1989, p 33.

about the cotton and linen yarn they were using to make cloth for printing in 1768-9. This was all hand-spun and so was probably similar to what had been used to make cloth for printing since 1736. In 1768-9 their 'Common Grey' (or bleached white) cloth was made in 28-yard long pieces about 1 yard wide and costing 22s – 23s a piece. It was made of 10 – 15 count cotton, that is 10 – 15 hanks of cotton yarn together weighing 1lb. This cost 2s 3d – 2s 4d per lb, when the price of raw cotton was 13d per lb. so the spinning cost 14d or 15d per lb. The linen yarn used was of a similar coarse quality. They also made 'Fine Grey' (or white) at 29 - 30s a piece. This was made from 16 – 20 count cotton worth 2s 7d - 3s per lb (so costing 18 - 23d to spin), and a finer linen warp.[103]

These were the grades of cotton and linen that were normally spun by hand spinners.[104] It was always possible for a few, especially deft, women to spin finer yarn, but the time taken and therefore the price rose steeply as the yarn became finer. The average spinner took perhaps 2 days to clean, card, rove and spin 1lb of 12s and 3 days to do 1lb of 20s. The highly skilled spinner probably took 1 1/3 days for 12s and 2 days for 20s. She needed 5 days for 30s and 12 days for 40s. Although water-frames worked more slowly on fine work than on coarser work, the costs rose only modestly and the quantity they could produce was unlimited. Thus the supply of fine yarn was no longer strictly limited to the output of a very few, highly skilled women. Suddenly, from 1774 onwards, a new type of cotton cloth became available to the printers.

To recap, printing cotton had become an important activity in Europe from 1660 to 1721 and was based on Indian and other oriental technology. It was always done on the imported pure cotton cloth known as calico, so the activity became known for several centuries as 'calico printing'. In England the printers were not allowed to print on imported calico for home sales after 1721, but after 1736 they were allowed to print on English-made

---

[103] John Rylands Library, GB 133 Eng MS 1199, their stock-take.
[104] Liverpool Record Office, Nicholson papers 920 NIC 5/5; Aspin, 1964, p 44; Hills, 1970, p 19.

linen/cotton cloth (which had linen warp and cotton weft). This was much less satisfactory because it was coarse and the linen did not take dye easily. However the demand for brightly printed cottons was irrepressible and the printers greatly improved their technology.[105] The demand for printed cloth for sale in Britain was mainly responsible for the large increase in cotton manufacture between 1736 and 1774. After 1774 it became possible to make pure cotton cloth in England using the strong warp made by the water-frame. It also became possible to make much finer cloth. These two developments were quickly reflected in the activities of Cardwell, Birley. In 1768-9 they were producing almost entirely the two grades of linen/cotton cloth described above. They had about £4,600-worth of these cloths in stock at the year-end while they had only £170-worth of 'superfine' cloth made with 28 count cotton. By 1777 they had started making 'calico' (all cotton cloth). 'Common' cloth had almost disappeared and 'superfines' were becoming more important. By 1781 calicos were more numerous in their stock than linen/cotton cloths and by 1783 their production had gone over entirely to calicos. These calicos were all much finer than the linen/cottons had been. The cotton yarn in stock in 1784 ranged from 20s to 30s.[106]

This increased demand for finer cotton cloth triggered the third famous development. Samuel Crompton, born Dec 1753, worked on a jenny in Bolton around 1770 as well as learning to weave. In 1774 he started experimenting to try and spin finer yarn. His 'Mule', as it came to be called, was completed in 1779. He produced fine yarn and was paid 14s for 1 lb of No 80.[107] This was a huge leap from the 30s and 40s which had been regarded as 'best superfine'. No 80 was gossamer fine. In 1780 he showed his machine to most of the major cotton manufacturers. It was only a prototype but it was very quickly improved upon by many different engineers so that by the mid-1780s hundreds of 'mules' were producing a new product – British-made muslins or fine cotton

---

[105] Chapman & Chassagne, 1981, pp 10 – 21.
[106] John Rylands Library GB 133 Eng MS 1199.
[107] French, 1859, pp 54 & 62.

cloth.[108]   This rapid development was made possible because
Crompton did not take out a patent. This was partly because he did
not have enough capital to enable him to obtain and enforce a
patent and partly because patents were not popular in Lancashire.
This was probably due to the important position of Quakers and
Unitarians in the business community. Quakers kept clear of the
law because they felt that 'truth was not found' in courts.
Unitarians were less severe but lawyers were few in the
Manchester-Liverpool area because neither town had law courts.
Both groups stressed the importance of ensuring benefits for the
whole community and not just for individuals. Preston, on the
other hand, where Arkwright was brought up, was described by
Defoe in 1724: 'Here's no manufacture. The town is full of
attorneys, proctors and notaries.'[109] The list of five 'pirates' of the
1769 patent, against whom Arkwright contemplated legal action in
1782 – including Peel, Drinkwater and Morley – shows that patents
did not have universal approval.[110]

To return to 1774. There were two legal problems with British-
made, pure cotton cloth. It was probably illegal under the 1721
Act, and was liable to a double Excise Tax. Need and Strutt,
without Arkwright, negotiated with MPs to try and get this
situation changed and Strutt appeared before a House of Commons
Committee. A new Act was passed in June 1774 removing both
problems. The road was then clear for the manufacture of British
calico. 57,000 yards were produced in 1775 and by 1783 the
amount had leapt to 3.6 million yards. This golden future had
apparently been obscure to Arkwright at the beginning. During
1774 the partners' two factories had worked full-time supplying the
hosiery industry and presumably it had been thought that they were
supplying very nearly the whole of the market. In the partnership
accounts to November 1774 *they had evidently made over £4,000
clear profit*, so Arkwright proposed to Need and Strutt that they
buy his share of the partnership and pay him his share of about

---

[108] Unwin, 1968, pp 15 – 16.
[109] Defoe, Daniel, 1991 ed., p 290. Preston was the seat of the Lancashire
Palatinate Courts.
[110] Fitton, 1989, p 100.

£1,000 *per annum* for the life of the patent. An agreement to this effect was made out and signed in Nov 1774. Perhaps he soon recognized his mistake and realized that there was a huge extra market for their yarn for making calico because by early 1775 he had made a verbal agreement with Need and Strutt *not* to execute the November agreement.

At this stage we arrive at the great mystery of the Arkwright story. Three years earlier two of the other participants had died - Brown, the watch-maker, in November 1771, and Thornley, one of the three original partners, in January 1772. Thornley's widow had sold his share. Smalley had returned from Preston with his family in 1774 to manage the mill, but he and Arkwright soon quarrelled and Arkwright seems to have wanted to drive him away. Arkwright seems to have decided that every effort should be made to extend the patent cover so as to reap the harvest of the calico market. His idea seems to have been that they should get a new patent to cover the carding and roving machinery they used in their two factories. A patent granted in 1775 (as one actually was) would extend their monopoly for about six more years. It would seem that Strutt and Need did not agree with this. If there was any 'intellectual property' in their designs for this machinery it would appear to have belonged to all the partners as it must have been 'invented' either by one or more of the partners or by their employees. We know that many people, including Hargreaves in Nottingham, had been experimenting and using carding and roving machinery since 1768.

Yet what happened was that in early 1775 Arkwright was discussing with his lawyers whether he alone could patent the carding and roving machinery they used.[111] *It does not seem possible to make sense of this without assuming that this must have been part of an agreement with Strutt and Need that he made around the end of 1774. The existence of such an agreement would explain why Strutt and Need were not included in the patent of 1775 for this carding and roving machinery, and why Strutt did not appear for either side and was not even mentioned in the various*

---

[111] Fitton, 1989, pp 40-41.

lawsuits over this patent that took place between 1781 and 1785 while he was still alive. Strutt's wife died in 1774 and he was so affected by her loss that although he continued to work he became a social recluse. This left Arkwright to publicize their achievements - a role which he enjoyed. Arkwright and Strutt sued Mr James, Hargreaves' old partner, who replaced Hargreaves' machines with water-frames in 1777-8 without taking a license under the 1769 patent. They won a judgement in their favour just before the patent expired in 1783. James paid nominal damages.[112] Strutt and Arkwright remained friends and William Strutt was one of Arkwright's executors. Indeed it seems likely that there was a third part to the agreement of late 1774 to the effect that the old partnership should own only the 1769 patent, the two existing factories and the new mill at Cromford, for which they had already started to build the half-mile long tunnel needed for its outfall. This second, larger factory at Cromford was not completed until 1776. It seems likely that there was also a fourth part to this agreement. This was that they should try and get Smalley to retire and then the three remaining partners should each separately finance whatever mills they liked, using all the machines they had developed. This, anyway, was what happened. Strutt built his own mills at Belper and Milford and Arkwright built several for himself. Such a complex agreement may have remained verbal and that may be the reason why there is no record of it.

Smalley left the partnership in February 1777 and Need died in 1781. The negotiations with Smalley valued his one-fifth share of the partnership at £1,200 a year until 1783 when the patent was due to expire and a sum of £3,200 for his share of the capital in the business as shown in the November 1776 'Annual Settlement'. *These figures indicate that the partners were able to take out a total of about £6,000 p.a. by 1776 which makes Arkwright's idea of taking £1,000 p.a. in 1774 look reasonable. If £3,200 was a one-fifth share, the partners' equity was about £16,000 in 1776. This suggests that, in 1774, when Strutt saw the House of Commons Committee and mentioned the figure of £13,000, it represented the partners' equity at that time. This was much more than the £1,000*

---

[112] Fitton, 1989, pp 103-4.

*- £1,200 that the partners had invested (see above p. 89) in January
1770. Substantial profits of about £12,000 must have been made
and reinvested in the business between 1771 and 1774. The
factories were probably highly profitable from the beginning. The
Nottingham mill may have made £2,000 p.a. for the four years
1771 – 74 and Cromford perhaps made £2,000 p.a. in 1773-74.*
That would produce the £12,000 needed. That profits on this scale
were earned by water-frame mills in the early years is shown in the
description of the Papplewick Mill in Nottinghamshire in 1784.[113]
This estimates weekly sales of 200 times £2 18s 5d, equalling
approximately £30,000 p.a., and weekly costs (including raw
cotton) of 200 times £1 10s 1d which would equal approximately
£15,000 p.a. This would imply an annual profit, before financial
expenses and partners' salaries, of over £14,000 p.a. This high
profitability appears to have been partly the result of the
traditionally high prices for finer yarn.

After this description of the principal events in the development of
mechanized spinning what can we say about the process of
innovation? First, did it occur in 'centres of competence or
excellence'? The prototypes made by Hargreaves and Crompton
were mainly concerned with techniques to draw out the fibres of
the cotton, with just enough twist to hold the thread together before
twisting it and winding it up. Both men were thoroughly
experienced in cotton spinning and came from the heart of the
cotton-manufacturing area. The success of their prototypes as
production machines depended on their development into reliable
machinery. This was the work of the precision-mechanical
engineering community of the South Lancashire area: people who
had previously made watches, clocks and tools. By the mid-18th
century they were making virtually all the watch movements
produced in Britain, large numbers of sets of clock parts and all the
tools used in this work. They turned, drilled, threaded and filed
metal very accurately, and understood how to fit the parts of
rotating machines. These people have not been mentioned much in
traditional historical accounts. However Adam Smith, writing in
1776, noted that they had reduced the cost of watch movements

---

[113] Nottingham Record Office DD4P 79/63.

from about £20 in around 1650 to £1 in the 1770s.[114] Their tools can be examined in J. Wyke's catalogue, 1758 – 1782.[115] They were part of a larger community of metal-working craftsmen, which included whitesmiths, blacksmiths, wire-workers, casters, braziers et al., that had grown up on the Lancashire coalfield. We can get an approximate idea of how numerous they were from the archives of Arley Hall, Cheshire, an agricultural estate with three corn mills, 15 miles south of a coal mine. In the Index on its website are more than 500 invoices from metal-working firms dated between 1750 and 1790 as shown in Table 9.[116] The glossary to this Index describes some of them in greater detail:

---

[114] Smith, 1776, Book 1, Chap XI, Part 3, p 243.
[115] Wyke. 1978.
[116] Arley Hall Archives website.

Table 9   Metal-working firms invoicing the Arley Estate
1750 - 90

Iron Trades	Iron merchants	3
	Iron casters	2
	Iron forgers	1
	Nail seller	7
	Iron mongers	18
	Blacksmiths	26
	Slitting and rolling mill	1
Non-ferrous trades	Brazier & whitesmith	6
	Tinman, tinsmith, pewterer	7
	Plumber	9
Machinery makers	Millwrights	6
	Pump-makers	5
	Tool-makers	3
	Wire-workers	2
	Machine-makers	3
Clock-makers		9
Wheelwrights & coach makers		10
Total		119

An interesting example of the development of this community is provided by William Cannan. He was a carpenter who came from Scotland and settled among the craftsmen in the little coal-mining and metal-working community at Atherton (then called Chowbent), 5 miles south-west of Bolton. He probably entered the textile machinery business by making parts for spinning wheels. No doubt he made Jennies in the 1770s. Between 1780 and 1784 he took on four young Scottish relations as apprentices and showed them how to make 'Mules'. These four men, Adam and George Murray, James McConnell and John Kennedy, became some of the greatest developers and operators of spinning machinery in Lancashire.[117] Arkwright's team effectively included three men from this world - Highs who did the original design, and Kay and Brown who built the first machines. His team also included people, most notably Strutt, who came from the other area in Britain that had been making complex machinery since the 17th Century – the framework-knitting machine makers of Nottingham, Derby and Leicester. The knitting machine consisted of more than 2000 components. It had been invented by the Rev. William Lee in about 1589 but was not transformed by engineers into a reliable, commercial machine until about 1650.[118]

These two areas had the best precision-mechanical engineering craftsmen in Britain. It was due to them that the water-frame was such a revolutionary success. Arkwright's archive seems not to contain any papers about his technical interests – unlike those of two other famous inventors, Watt and Wedgwood – so it seems unlikely that he made a great technical contribution. However, he deserves credit for getting together a team of technical people and finding the financial backing to keep them working for more than three years, until a factory was built that produced a product which found such a large and profitable market. In engineering terms, spinning with rollers was an obvious idea that had been thought of and tried by several people (including Paul and Wyatt), but making reliable working machinery was another matter. Crompton also used rollers but the water-frame was a machine built principally by engineers and their design was unable to correct the fact that 'roller-drafting attenuates the thin places' in the yarn, so that it was not possible to make yarn finer than 50 or 60 count on this machine. Crompton and Hargreaves, as experienced spinners, knew that 'drafting against twist attenuates the thicker places'.[119] In Crompton's machine the cotton was drawn out by rollers on to spindles on a moving carriage. It was so effective because 'when

---

[117] Oxford Archaeology North 2007 for A. & G. Murray; Lee, 1972.

[118] Lewis, 1986, pp 129 - 148.

[119] Catling, 1978, p 35.

the carriage had been pulled out nearly to the end of its run, the rollers were stopped and the lengths of cotton between the rollers and the spindles would be stretched to even them out *either* in the last few inches of the draw after the rollers had stopped *or* after the carriage had stopped and the spindles continued to be twisted.'[120] This was what enabled his machine to spin fine yarn with counts of 100 or even 500, and illustrates that a detailed knowledge of both precision-engineering and cotton-spinning was required for the development of effective cotton-spinning machinery. It was no accident that advanced spinning machinery was first made in Lancashire as that was where centres of excellence in both these fields existed.

The trigger that made the development of mechanical spinning so desirable in the late 1760s was clearly the great shortage of hand-spinners compared with the rapidly increasing demand for cotton cloth. The trigger to develop the spinning of finer yarn was, as we have seen, the demand of the calico printers for a finer cotton cloth. One could argue that it was the appearance of the triggers in the appropriate centres of excellence that caused the technical innovation, but this would be wrong because triggers are only inducements. They consist of information which may reach many people who make no use of it, or people who make a foolish use of it as in the example of Wyatt and Paul and their investors described above. It is only when information arrives in the appropriate 'centres of excellence', where there are individuals with the necessary skills, a small amount of capital to experiment with and the absence of family or other pressures that prevent them, that 'inventors' are created.

It is not only inventors but whole industries that require the appropriate centres of competence and excellence. For example in the early 1780s three rich men – Robert Brooke, Richard Talbot and Baron Hamilton – attempted to establish cotton-manufacturing in three places in Ireland. They were only a short sea journey from the many successful businesses in Lancashire but all their

---

[120] Hills, 1970, p 118.

enterprises quickly folded after huge losses.[121] What went wrong? They were not clever about hiring the right managers, but the over-arching problem was that Ireland was not like South Lancashire where coal was mined in many places. Round each mine in South Lancashire metal workers clustered – nailers, blacksmiths, braziers, whitesmiths, specializing in tin and solders, clockmakers and so on – to get the benefit of cheap coal. Every skill was available within a few miles and there were large numbers of people who had some experience of metal-working, of tools and machinery. In Ireland, by contrast, there were no coal mines, so it was a precision engineering desert. That, perhaps, was why David Clarke of Stockport, who went there and made textile machinery between 1780 and 1785, told the Parliamentary Committee in 1785 that he would never return to Ireland – 'I return thanks that I am here safe.'[122] Chris Aspin has provided another little story about an attempt to start cotton-spinning in continental Europe. In 1789 Francis Wheelhouse, a clock-maker aged 56, who had been running his own spinning mill for ten years on the Isle of Man, was 'decoyed to Portugal to spin for the Queen'. Actually they wanted him to run a cotton mill but he had to start by building it all by himself as there were no other skilled people in the country able to do it.[123]

What were the obstacles to the development of effective spinning machinery? The principal one was the hostility of the hand-spinners, their families and their communities, generated by the fear of losing their jobs. We have seen (pp 84-7 above) that Paul and Wyatt knew about this risk in 1736 and also how it dissuaded Earnshaw and Taylor – two men living in the cotton area and probably with the necessary engineering skills – from making machines in the 1750s. The most famous example is provided by the well-known riots of 1779 which destroyed Arkwright's factory at Birkacre and a Peel family factory at Altham in Lancashire, and caused Crompton to hide his prototype in the roof.[124] The riots

---

[121] Aspin, 2010, pp 16-36.
[122] Lambert, 1976, pp 208-10.
[123] Aspin, 2011.
[124] Wadsworth & Mann, 1931, p 448.

spread over a large region in Lancashire and Cheshire, from Preston and Blackburn in the north through Wigan, Warrington, Bolton, Bury and Stockport, and continued from 27 Sep to 13 Oct. As many as 5,000 rioters were assembled in some places and by the end nineteen companies of foot soldiers and six troops of horse were engaged in trying to prevent further damage. The riots caused the Peels to move this part of their operations out of the cotton area to Burton-on-Trent.[125] That the cause of the unemployment sparking the riot was a war-time trade depression and not the new machinery only emphasises the strength of feeling on the issue.[126] The violence of this reaction to unemployment shows that the peaceful introduction of the Jenny and early carding machines in Lancashire was only achieved by the maintenance of good employment levels in the 1770s. If these had been the only new textile machines they probably would not have survived a period of prolonged unemployment. It was the revolution created by the water-frame and the mule that ensured that textile machinery was a lasting innovation.

As we have seen Arkwright took his team to Nottingham where there were virtually no cotton-spinners, but where there was a substantial demand for cotton yarn for the local framework-knitting industry, so there were six-and-a-half years – mid 1768 to the end of 1774 – before the existence of his machinery became known to many hand cotton-spinners. These years of peaceful development and the location of most of the early mills in Nottinghamshire and Derbyshire were two important factors. If a large water-powered mill, full of spinning machinery, working 24 hours per day and manned principally by children, had appeared in the main cotton area in the early 1770s, it might well have sparked so much hostility that the history of mechanization would have been different. Yarn from Arkwright's machines started to appear in the traditional cotton-manufacturing areas in 1773; it was used to provide, not only the weft but also the warp for the new, pure cotton cloth. This may have started to kindle the worries that came out in the 1779 riots and were then expressed in a well-known

---

[125] Chapman, 1969, pp 64 – 5.
[126] Rose, 1963, pp 78 –89.

pamphlet which alleged that each patent machine, attended by a child, did as much work as used to employ ten adults. [127] However, in the 1780s the Water-Frame and the Mule so transformed cotton manufacturing that a return to hand methods was unthinkable.

The conclusion, then, seems to be that the mechanization of cotton spinning was triggered by the persistent serious shortage of cotton spinners. It was made possible by the existence of a precision-mechanical engineering industry in Lancashire and Nottingham, close to the location of a community experienced in cotton-spinning and manufacturing. The potential problems created by the destruction of jobs by mechanization were partly solved by developing and working the machinery in the early stages at a safe distance from the traditional hand cotton-spinners and partly by the huge growth in demand for cotton textiles. These conclusions perhaps also explain why the machinery was not developed anywhere else in the world. It seems that, at that time, these areas of England had a more sophisticated technology than anywhere else in Europe.

R.C.Allen has argued that the inventions were made in England because it was a high wage economy which therefore provided the best return on the capital invested in the machinery.[128] It is certainly true that the first jennies, with only 8 or 16 spindles, would not have been economic elsewhere. Their modest increase in production would not have provided a return on the capital cost when wages were lower. But the unpatented jennies were improved very quickly and in 1780, after the riots, the House of Commons was told that 'machines worked by one person can manufacture as much cotton yarn as nine persons can do by hand.' Furthermore 'a spinner on a single spindle earns 3d - 4d a day but working upon a jenny can now get 2s to 2s 6d a day.'[129] (2s = 24d, so 24 - 30d is 6 - 10 times 3d - 4d.) This suggests that Allen's estimate of the increase in productivity of jennies at only three times is understated. He compounds his problems by using the

---

[127] Mather, (anon.) 1780.
[128] Allen, 2009, pp 190 - 216.
[129] Journal of the House of Commons, vol 37, pp 925 - 6.

perfectly correct fact that the average woman only spun for 40% of her working day. Most mothers had lots of other duties but teenage girls were full-time spinners before marriage and they were, of course, the operators of the expensive jennies. A wisp of evidence that may help to confirm this is that Aspin found that the jenny he made from Hargreaves' drawings was too small for an adult and apparently designed for a twelve-year-old girl. The truth seems to be that the productivity of jennies by 1780 was much greater than Allen suggests and they would have been profitable all over Europe. They were indeed introduced into the cotton-manufacturing area of Chemnitz, Saxony, in 1785. In 1804-10 there were 9,000 machines there with a total of 200,000 spindles. Water-frame machines arrived there in 1799 and mules in 1813.[130]

Allen's view that the much more costly water-frames were not a sufficiently profitable investment to be used in France is also curious. If there had been Frenchmen with the technical skills to make water-frames and mules and the willingness to invest, they could have gone to England and looked at the machines even if the English were not legally allowed to export them. A good tool-maker/engineer would have been able to make a working machine after studying the original for an hour or so (as all the manufacturers' engineers did after examining Crompton's mule). Then they could have returned to France and they could have made them and, with their labour at half the price of rates in England, they could have operated them and taken the European market away from the expensive English workers. That this didn't happen suggests that there were few French precision engineers. But the whole position in France was quite different from England. The laws against wearing and printing calicos were removed in France in 1759. Imports poured in especially from Switzerland, a centre of calico printing on linen/cotton and on pure cotton cloth imported from India. C.B.Oberkampf, who became the leading French calico printer, came from his father's Swiss works to Versailles in 1760. He printed on linen/cotton cloth from the Beaujolais and Rouen areas and also on pure cotton cloth from India - *guinees* and *baffetas* - imported by the English, French and Dutch East India

---

[130] Aspin, C., & Chapman, S.D., 1964, p 66.

companies. In 1782 he sampled Manchester calico and continued to buy that until 1792 (when supplies were cut off by the wars) and regarded 'their price and quality as his "standard" '.[131] With plenty of imported cloth available to the calico printers and English cotton yarn available to European cotton weavers, there was less incentive for Frenchmen to set up cotton-spinning mills. Water-frames and mules only penetrated into Europe very slowly and when they did it was usually with the help of English-trained engineers and managers. Outside Europe precision mechanical engineering was almost non-existent. Also, from what has been said above about the spinners' fear of unemployment, it seems unlikely that even the simplest jenny would have survived in India or China where there were millions of hand-spinners keen to protect their jobs.

In the 19th and 20th centuries people became familiar with the fact that new machinery can cause mass unemployment. But in 1780 such things had never happened. Normally, mechanical improvements had merely reduced part of the labour in some people's work. The Water-frame and the Mule were the first two of a series of machines that changed the world for good. By the early 1780s cotton-spinning by hand in England had disappeared. Soon after 1800, in the whole of Europe, there can have been few cotton-spinners, working by hand, left. After 1820, tens of thousands of hand-loom weavers were made redundant in Lancashire by power looms and, overseas, cloth spun and woven by machine was destroying the employment of hundreds of thousands who had grown, spun and woven cotton goods for centuries. However they were largely in India, the Middle East and Latin America where Europeans did not much notice them. This was why what happened in North-West England in the 1770s and 1780s was an industrial revolution. Wealth was created but there was social cost. One reason why machinery was eventually introduced all over the world was to recover the employment in textile manufacture that had been lost to machine-made imports from Britain and other countries with machines. Imports from England destroyed the Indian cotton industry to such an extent that, in the 1830s, the Governor-General could write that 'the bones of

---

[131] Chapman, S.D., Chassagne S., 1981, pp 109, 125 and 156-63.

the cotton-weavers are bleaching the plains of India'.[132] Modern factories full of machinery were introduced into India in the 1850s, by which time there were few hand-workers still trying to compete with the standard grades of machine-made cloth that were being imported.

It is important to notice that it was from among the skilled workers that the famous macro-inventors appeared, as the lives of the three 'inventors' involved in the mechanization of spinning show. James Hargreaves was a craftsman. He may have had some ownership rights (and hence some capital) in the cottage and its land where he lived with his family. His family continued to live there until 1882.[133] His two sons, aged 25 and 17 in 1767, were weaving there, and three daughters aged over 15 were no doubt spinning. Three or more younger children would have kept his wife busy. So there was a good income coming into the household which probably had much in common with that of the Lathams whose account book has survived.[134] This was why Hargreaves had the time and money to experiment with his spinning machine. He and his family were contractors supplying Peel with cloth for his calico-printing business. Peel supplied the linen warps and raw cotton and they sold him cloth at piece-rate prices, in the same way that Cardwell, Birley were operating. Samuel Crompton came from a similar background but he was only in his early twenties when he experimented with his machine.

Richard Arkwright was also a craftsman. His ancestors, fully described by Fitton, sometimes owned a few houses in Preston and so he probably inherited at least part of the small capital he would have needed to set up as a barber and get married. His first father-in-law lent him £60 which he was unable to repay until he had access to his second wife's modest capital.[135] He had enough money to employ John Kay for about six months making the first machine – perhaps £20 - £30. His first two partners, Smalley and

[132] Riello, 2009, pp 400 –1.
[133] Aspin, 1964, p 9.
[134] Foster, 2002, pp 142-171.
[135] Fitton, 1989, p 9, note 2.

Thornley, invested perhaps around £200 each but Thornley had to ask Smalley to pay his last instalment. Strutt was apprenticed as a wheelwright and became involved with framework-knitting machines in his twenties. In 1754, when he was 28, he inherited a small farm from an uncle. He then married Elizabeth Woolat whom he had known for a long time. She worked for several Unitarian ministers. These men probably introduced her husband to the richer businessmen who helped him commercialize the 'Derby Rib', an attachment to the framework-knitting machine which made his fortune.

The skills of people in the North-West (Lancashire, Cheshire, Staffordshire, the West Riding of Yorkshire and surrounding areas) had developed as a result of the particular wealth distribution and business culture which had arisen there. There had for some time been a large number of families with some capital. As we have seen, in the 1660s, in the Northwich Hundred of Cheshire and the Blackburn Hundred of Lancashire, perhaps two-thirds of families had some capital (see above p.73). This situation had developed by the end of the 16th century and lasted into the 19th Century.[136] The Arley Hall invoices 1750-90 [137] show large numbers of families of skilled men - farmers, carpenters, plumbers, etc. - in business on their own account. They were not people without capital who needed to be paid at the end of each week or month for the work they had done. Many only sent in their invoices several months or even a year after they had done their work. This may have been partly because they knew that money owed by the Warburtons was like money in a bank - available to you at any time you sent to ask for it - and just as secure. It is also evidence of the possession of significant capital. Some of these families had a few thousand pounds – a considerable sum for the time. Robert Peel (1723 – 95) inherited a farm worth about £2,000 and Jedediah Strutt received a smaller one. Both started doing practical manual work but by developing a business finally made fortunes of hundreds of thousands of pounds. The three famous cotton inventors all had capital of less than £200 before their innovations, but they were

---

[136] Foster, 2004, pp 44 – 60, pp 146 – 165, p 303; Foster, 1992, pp 11 – 14.
[137] Arley Hall Archive website.

craftsmen who were not taking instructions from anyone and they each had enough to support their families while experimenting with their ideas. It was in the many thousands of families of this kind that all these skills developed. The system of apprenticeships has left few records in the North-West but we know that families tried to train their children in some business and give each a portion. Large numbers of people were competing to do something better than the person next door and the vigour of the society was based on this great competition. It was the wide distribution of wealth and the business culture that created and encouraged the competition, from which the mechanical innovations derived.

Mokyr has made a powerful case for the importance of the Enlightenment and the Scientific Revolution in the inventiveness of the Industrial Revolution. He discusses the advantage that Britain had in the 18th century from the large number of skilled workers in metal-working and many other trades.[138] He describes them as 'the unsung foot-soldiers of the Industrial Revolution', 'craftsmen blessed by a natural dexterity who possessed a technical savoir-faire taught in no school'. They certainly benefited from the experimenting spirit and there was also a sort of partnership between the Scientific Revolution and practical craftsmen. The scientists often needed equipment for their experiments and craftsmen made it for them. They got to know each other and ideas were exchanged. An interesting early example of the varied ways this partnership worked is provided by Jeremiah Horrocks. He was the grandson of Thomas Aspinall, who is thought to have brought watch-making to Liverpool, and the son of his apprentice James Horrocks, so he must have been brought up amidst watch-makers. He went to Emmanuel College Cambridge and learnt astronomy which was an important subject for people making time-pieces because 'Sun' and 'clock' time are different. Horrocks is famous for his observation of the Transit of Venus in 1639. He was friends with William Crabtree and William Gascoigne, who is usually credited with the invention of the micrometer-controlled telescope eye-piece which allowed very accurate small measurements. Since this depended on very accurately cut, fine threads, which could

---

[138] Mokyr, 2009, pp 106-13.

only have been done at this period by the highest quality watch-makers, its connection with the business of the Aspinall/Horrocks family is very likely.[139]

Academic people may find it easier to credit important wealth creations to their colleagues but we know that the innovations of Microsoft, Google and Facebook (for example) were all made in the bedrooms and garages of young men, rather than in the research laboratories of professors. But the young people had read the professors' books and had attended a few of their lectures, so we can all believe in a partnership in which there must be many pupils, as only a few will make innovations.

7 The growth of European wealth creation to 1820

In Maddison's *per capita* GDP figures for 1700 the Netherlands is shown as the leader in Europe with $2,130, a rise of 54% since 1600. Its world-wide trade and its plantations overseas, together with its technical leadership in many manufactures, had enabled its small, homogenous population, with their widely owned wealth, to prosper greatly. The UK figures had also increased, but only by 28% so at $1,250 it was 59% of the figure for Holland. The West European average had increased by 12% to $997. Italy had remained stationary at $1,100 and France, under the '*Roi Soleil*', and Germany, with its autocratic princes now firmly established, both lagged behind at $910.

Holland and England shared two experiences in the 17th century. Both founded East India Companies, which started trading with India and the Far East and established plantations in the Americas and the Caribbean. Englishmen also settled in significant numbers in North America. These overseas ventures brought a large number of new substances to Europe and this trading was a major element in the creation of new wealth in both countries. The second experience the two countries shared was the struggle against autocratic monarchs who tried to crush their independence. Holland had to defend itself against Spain on and off for much of the second half of the 16th century and for the first fifty years of

---

[139] Bailey, 1969, pp 1 – 15; Aughton, 2004; Chapman, 2007, pp 19 – 40.

the 17th century. In England Charles I found the experience of sharing power with Parliament on the model inherited from Elizabeth's reign to be intolerable. He tried to govern without Parliament, and when that experiment got into difficulties he allied himself with the great majority of the peers and the old landed gentry and arrayed his party in arms. The new middle-income families, which had come into existence as we have seen since 1550, rallied to support Parliament. They were led by the business community in London and the Home counties and got support from textile-manufacturing populations in East Anglia, the West Riding of Yorkshire and Lancashire, and metal-workers in the East and West Midlands.[140] They successfully opposed Charles I and won the Civil War.

In 1648 when the war in Europe and the Civil War in England were ended the British business community, now under the Commonwealth, decided that it would be national policy to have a flourishing merchant navy. The Navigation Acts, 1651, were therefore passed restricting the carriage of imports to Britain and its colonies to British ships and those of the nation that had produced the imported goods. This was an attack on their fellow businessmen in Holland who until then had had the major share of moving all the cargoes in Western Europe. This led to two Anglo-Dutch naval wars in the 1650s and 1660s and it did damage to Dutch business. Nevertheless in 1688 the English were very pleased to accept the help of the Dutch and William of Orange to change their monarchy. In return both nations fought as allies to repel the French invasion of Holland. If any of the autocratic monarchs had been successful in their wars it would probably have caused a serious decline in the ability of the European peoples to increase their wealth.

However Dutch economic growth and wealth creation faltered in the 18th century. The underlying cause seems to have been the concentration of capital in urban oligarchies of patricians who also had most of the political power. There were two key aspects to this. First they had many of the best jobs. 'After 1660 the

---

[140] Gardiner, 1888; Map of England, Sep 1643.

Patriciate tightened its grip on income-generating public offices'.[141]
Not only did members of the Patriciate enjoy income from
appointments like burgomaster, these jobs also provided access to
additional offices, good contracts and profitable investment
opportunities. Secondly, they owned much of the existing capital
in the shape of the huge state debts built up to finance the wars
from 1672 - 1713. These bonds were mainly held by the oligarchs
and often comprised 50% - 60% of their wealth. 'After 1713
interest payments absorbed 70% of Holland's tax revenues.'[142] If
the oligarchs had paid tax to finance the wars, rather than making
loans, their wealth would have been reduced. This is an example of
oligarchs using their political power to concentrate wealth in their
own hands. The effect of this concentration of wealth on the ability
of the society to generate technical and commercial innovations can
be seen in the performance of the cotton industry.

Indian cottons poured into Holland after 1670 as they did into
France and England but, unlike the position in these last two
countries, no legal restrictions were enacted in Holland. The calico
printing industry got going just north of Amsterdam and became
one of the city's largest, with thirty-four firms operating in 1735
employing thousands of workers. They were able to print all the
time on the most suitable Indian cotton which the Dutch East India
Company (the V.O.C.) could import direct at minimum cost. After
1721 the English industry was not allowed to print for the home
market on Indian cloth and after 1736 they had to struggle with the
half linen/half cotton cloth made in Lancashire. The Dutch industry
peaked with around 80 firms in 1750 and had virtually disappeared
by 1780. The English and other firms in Switzerland, Germany
and France massively improved their printing technology, which
lowered prices. This created the huge demand for printed cotton
cloth that in turn drove the requirement to mechanize the
production of cotton yarn. It could all have happened in Holland
but the innovative spirit derived from the many small capitalists
then existing there, that had put up a forest of windmills just north
of Amsterdam to drive powered saws after 1596, was missing in

---

[141] De Vries & Van der Woude, p 588.
[142] De Vries & Van der Woude, pp 591 & 682.

the 18th century. These saws had been used to cut the Scandinavian logs into the planks that made the famous 'fluteships' that dominated west European shipping in the 17th century. These powered saws were far ahead of anything similar in Europe but were only one of many innovations that made the Dutch so much richer than people in the rest of Europe in the 17th century.[143]

By 1820 the European miracle of wealth creation was beginning to get underway. The many innovations, mostly pioneered in the UK - in machinery, steam engines, coal-firing and agricultural improvements - had combined with the new political climate, created by the French Revolution, to set more people free to innovate. West European wealth had improved by 20% to a *per capita* average of $1,202. The figure for the UK had increased by 36% to $1,706. Maddison has provided an additional figure showing Britain, excluding Ireland, at $2,122. Britain was the richest country in Europe, ahead of the Netherlands, which had sunk to $1,838. France and Germany had increased by 24% and 18% respectively, but Germany's wealth was only just over half that of Britain.

The best known explanation of the causes of wealth creation is the Weber/Tawney thesis, giving prominence to the 'Protestant Ethic'. That approach gets little support from Maddison: Italy became a much richer country than any other in Europe between 1000 and 1500 and then remained stationary. It remained Catholic throughout. However it has been briefly mentioned that, during their best periods of growth, North Italian, South German and Lancashire societies were associated with new religious groups. These groups emerged in those societies after the wealth-redistributing events that contributed to their creation. Thus, in North Italy, the new religious groups became active in the 12th century, whereas the towns had started to grow large in the 11th century. In South Germany the preachers, who sparked the War of 1525, came later than the big redistribution which began before 1400. In Lancashire the rise of Bolton, as the 'Geneva of the North', was late Elizabethan, not early in the 16th century. The

---

[143] De Vries & Van der Woude, pp 297 - 8 & 633.

new religious groups seem to be a part of the cultures of these societies rather than the cause of the new business activity, as Weber and Tawney suggested.

It is useful in conclusion to review our three societies and Maddison's figures. In the first period, from 1000 to 1500, Italy was the most successful with a growth in *per capita* GDP of 144%, as compared with a West European average increase of only 80% (see Table 10 below). We have also seen the break-up of these arrangements, the concentration of political power from the 14th Century onwards, and a small rich group gaining most of the wealth. *Per capita* wealth may have been larger in 1350 than it was in 1500. Certainly it did not increase further in the following three centuries up to 1820.

Table 10 The growth of *per capita* GDP in 5 areas
(1990 International dollars)

	AD 1000	AD 1500	% inc	AD 1600	% inc	AD 1700	% inc	AD 1820	% inc
Italy	450	1100	144	1,100	Nil	1,100	nil	1,117	nil
Belgium	425	875	105	976	11	1,144	17	1,319	24
Netherlands	425	761	79	1,328	81	2,130	54	1,838	-14
U.K.	400	714	79	974	36	1,250	28	1,706	36
West European average	427	771	80	889	15	997	11	1,202	20

Source: Maddison, 2007

Maddison's figures for Germany (Table 1 above) are always below the West European average. The innovative spirit there between 1350 and 1500 failed to register and was never accompanied by strong plural political institutions. But these figures illustrate another characteristic of Maddison's geographical method. In most of the first six centuries of his analysis the Low Countries – a group of small duchies – were part of the Holy Roman Empire, close to Charlemagne's old capital at Aachen, on the present borders of Belgium and France. As Table 10 shows, Belgium was the second most active area up to 1500 with a growth of 105%. The arrival of autocratic government there in the second half of the 16th century reduced its growth to 11% in the century up till 1600. The Netherlands, where wealth remained widely distributed and the political institutions plural, took over and recorded growth of 81% and 54% in the centuries to 1600 and 1700, against a West European average of 15% and 11%. The performance of the UK, including Lancashire, in the century up till 1600 at 36% was well below the Netherlands' figure of 81% and continued to be poor up to 1700 with a gain of only 28%, compared with the Netherlands' gain of 54%. The two countries were far ahead of the European average. What went wrong in Holland in the 18th century has been briefly discussed above (pp 110-112). We have seen that the main technical and commercial innovations were made in the three 'lead' countries – North Italy, the Netherlands and the UK, but the rest of Europe also grew slowly richer. One part of this was simply the mathematical effect on the average of the rise in the leaders. Another part was probably that the rest shared the new benefits in two ways. New products, like quinine or Indian cottons, also came to the European countries that did not trade overseas, as did the sugar, coffee, cotton and so on grown in Dutch, French or English plantations abroad. New technical improvements, as in glass manufacture and metal-casting, spread across Europe.

My thesis is that the structure of societies - their wealth distribution, institutions and culture - determine their economic performance. Other economists have noticed the importance of plural political institutions, but have not mentioned that, in the long term, these depend on a wide distribution of wealth.[144] Since 1945 the West has claimed that, to be 'acceptable' other societies should be democratic, with much emphasis on the importance of holding free elections. However, many authoritarian regimes, who go through the motions of having elections, have actually developed

---

[144] Acemoglu & Robinson, 2012.

methods for manipulating them. I would suggest that the existence of a wide distribution of wealth in a society should replace the presence of elections as the principal hall-mark of a 'good' society. How should wealth distribution be measured? The 'Gini co-efficient' seems not to have attracted the public's affections. National governments do not publicly attempt to chart global wealth distribution. *Forbes* Magazine is the leader in this. Even if a simple way of measuring the distribution were devised would it come into use? Thirty years ago Western societies all had quite a wide distribution of wealth, but inequality has grown and it appears that the rich are yet again trying to restrict the plurality of our institutions so that the model of a society which maintains a wider distribution of wealth and power is now being undermined from within.

The author ran a small precision engineering business that designed and made, and occasionally patented, special tools for telecommunications from 1970 to 1987. Since then he has spent time studying, sorting and cataloguing the Arley Estate records. He has written four books published by Arley Hall Press on the social and economic development of Cheshire and Lancashire 1500 - 1800 using these and many other archives.

Bibliography

(all books published in the UK except where noted)

Acemoglu, Daron, & Robinson, James A., 2012, *Why Nations Fail: the Origins of Power, Prosperity and Poverty.*

Aikin, J. (1795), *Description of the country from 30-40 miles around Manchester.*

Allen, Robert C. (1988), 'The Price of freehold land and the rate of interest in the seventeenth and eighteenth centuries', *Economic History Review*, 2nd Series, XLI, 1.

Allen, Robert C. (1992), *Enclosure and the Yeoman.*

Allen, Robert C. (2009), *The British Industrial Revolution in Global Perspective.*

Arley Hall Archives, www.arleyhallarchives.co.uk

Ashton, Thomas S. (1939), *An eighteenth century industrialist: Peter Stubbs of Warrington, 1756 - 1806.*

Aspin, Chris & Chapman, Stanley D. (1964), *James Hargreaves and the Spinning Jenny.*

Aspin, Chris (1968), "New Evidence of James Hargreaves", *Textile History* vol. 1/1, pp 119 – 21.

Aspin, Chris (2010), *The Unfortunate Philanthropists*, Helmshore Local History Society, 4 East St, Helmshore, Lancs, BB4 4JT.

Aspin, Chris (2011), *The Decoy*, Helmshore Local History Society.

Aughton, Peter (2004), *The Transit of Venus: the brief, brilliant life of Jeremiah Horrocks, father of British Astronomy.*

Bailey, F.A. and Barker, T.C. (1969), 'The 17th century origins of watch-making in south-west Lancashire' in Harris, John R., ed. *Liverpool and Merseyside.*

Baines, Edward (1835), *History of the Cotton Manufacture in Great Britain.*

Bannerjee, Abhijit, & Duflo, Esther (2011), *Poor Economics.*
BIOS Reporter (on line).

Blickle, P., (1981) *The Revolution of 1525: the German Peasants' War from a new perspective*, trans. Brady, T., & Midefort, E., (Baltimore).

Bliss, Mary (2003) 'The last years of John Ruddal, bell founder of Gloucester, 1828-35' in *Transactions of the Bristol & Gloucestershire Archaeological Society* 121, pp 11 - 22.

Borsay, Peter, ed. (1990), *The Eighteenth Century Town.*

Campbell, R. (1747), *The London Tradesman*, reprinted 1969, David & Charles.

Catling, Harold (1978), "The Development of the Spinning Mule", *Textile History*, vol. 9.

Chaloner, W.H. (1950 - 52), 'Charles Roe of Macclesfield, 1715-81; an eighteenth century industrialist', *Transactions of the Lancashire & Cheshire Antiquarian Society*, vol 62 (1950-1) for Pt 1. and vol 63 (1952-3) for Pt 2.

Chambers, J.D. (1932), *Nottinghamshire in the Eighteenth Century.*
Chapman, Alan (2007), 'Under a Lancashire Heaven', *Manchester Regional History Review,* vol 18.

Chapman, Stanley D. (1969), "The Peels in the Early English Cotton Industry", *Business History*, vol. 11, pp 64-5.

Chapman, Stanley D. & Chassagne, Serge (1981), *European Textile Printers in the Eighteenth Century – a study of Peel and Oberkampf.*

Chaudhuri, Kirt N. (1978), *The Trading World of Asia and the English East India Company 1660 - 1760.*

Chorley, P. (1987), 'The cloth exports of Flanders and northern France during the thirteenth century: a luxury trade?' *Economic History Review*, 2nd Series, XL, 3, pp 349-79.

Chorley, P. (1997), 'The evolution of the woollen 1300 - 1700' in Harte, N.B., ed. *The New Draperies in the Low Countries and England.*

CIBA Review, No 1 (1937)

CIBA Review, No 80 (1950), Edler de Roover, F., *Lucchese Silks.*

Cipolla, C.M. (1976), *Before the Industrial Revolution: European society and economy, 1000-1700.*

Collins, John (1682), *Salt and Fishery.*

Coster, Will (1999), 'Massacre and codes of conduct in the English Civil Wars' in Levene, Mark, & Robert, Penny, (eds) (1999, *The Massacre in History* (New York).

Crosby, A.G. (2008), 'The regional road network and the growth of Manchester in the 16th and 17th centuries', *Manchester Regional History Review*, vol 19.

Dallam, T., (1893), *Dallam's Travels 1599 - 1600*, Hakluyt Society, vol. 87.

Davis, R. (1961), 'England and the Mediterranean 1570-1670' in Fisher, F.J. (ed.) *Essays in the Economic and Social History of Tudor and Stuart England in honour of R.H.Tawney.*

Decker, Michael (2009), *Plants and Progress: Rethinking the Islamic Agricultural Revolution*, Journal of World History 20 No. 2, pp187-206

Defoe, Daniel (1991), *A Tour through the whole Island of Great Britain*, Yale Univ. Press, originally pub. 1726.

De Vries, Jan, & Van der Woude, Ad (1997), *The first modern economy: success, failure and perseverance of the Dutch economy 1500 - 1815.*

Edwards, M.M. (1967), *The Growth of the British Cotton Trade 1780 – 1815.*

Felkin, William (1867), *A History of the machine wrought hosiery and lace manufacture.*

Fischer, David H. (1989), *Albion's Seed. Four British folkways in America.*

Fitton, Robert S. & Wadsworth, Alfred P. (1958), *The Strutts and the Arkwrights 1758 – 1830. A study of the early factory system.*

Fitton, Robert S. (1989), *The Arkwrights: Spinners of Fortune.*

Foster, Charles F. (1992), *Four Cheshire Townships.*

Foster, Charles F. (1998), *Cheshire Cheese and Farming in the north-west in the 17th and 18th centuries.*

Foster, Charles F. (2002), *Seven Households: Life in Cheshire and Lancashire 1582 - 1774.*

Foster, Charles F. (2004), *Capital and Innovation: how Britain became the first Industrial Nation, a study of the Warrington, Knutsford, Northwich and Frodsham area 1500 – 1780.*

French, Gilbert J. (1859), *Life and Times of Samuel Crompton.*

Gardiner, Samuel R. (1886), *History of the Great Civil War,* vol i.

Gilboy, E. W. (1934), *Wages in Eighteenth Century England* (Harvard Univ. Press).

Grayson, A.J., & Jones, E.W. (1955), *Notes on the History of Wytham Estate with special reference to the Woodlands.*

Green, John Richard (1898), *A short history of the English People.*

Guest, Richard (1823), *A compendious History of the Cotton Manufacture.*

Guscott, S.J. (2003), 'Humphrey Chetham, 1580-1653', *Chetham Society* 3rd Series, vol. 45.

Hadfield, C. & Biddle, G. (1970), *The canals of north west England*, vol 1.

Hammond, Nigel (1974), *Rural Life in the Vale of the White Horse.*

Heller, Michael, G. (2009), *Capitalism, Institutions and Economic Development.*

Herlihy, D. (1958), *Pisa in the early Renaissance: a study of urban growth* (Yale Univ. Press).

Herlihy, D. (1967), *Medieval and Renaissance Pistoia* (Yale Univ. Press).

Herlihy, D. & Klapisch-Zuber. C. (1985), *Tuscans and their families: a study of the Florentine Catasto of 1427* (Yale Univ. Press).

Herlihy, D., Klapisch-Zuber, C., Litchfield, R.B., and Molho, A. (2002), (eds.) *Online Catasto of 1427*, Florentine Renaissance Resources (Providence).

Hills, Richard L. (1970), *Power in the Industrial Revolution.*

Jones, Eric L. (1974), *Agriculture and the Industrial Revolution.*

Jones, Eric L. (2009), 'Environmental effects of blood sports in Lowland England since 1750', *Rural History* 20 (1), pp 51 - 66.

Jones, Eric L. (2010), *Locating the Industrial Revolution: inducement and response* (Singapore).

Jones, Eric L. (2012), 'Gentry Culture and the Stifling of industry', in *Journal of Socioeconomics,* doi:10.1016/j.socec.2012.05.021

Jones, P.J. (1997), *The Italian City-State from Commune to Signoria.*

Jones, S.R. (1978), 'The development of needle manufacturing in the West Midlands before 1750', *Economic History Review*, 2nd Series, XXXI.

Journals of the House of Commons, vol 37.

Lambert, S. (1976) (ed.) *H of C Sessional Papers of the 18th Century,* Wilmington, Delaware, USA.

Landes, David S. (1983), *Revolution in time* (Harvard Univ. Press).

Landstrom, B. (1961), *The ship – a survey of the history of the ship … with reconstructions in words and pictures.*

Latham, Anthony J.H. (2009), 'Wigan 1540-1640: 'Pre-industrial growth and development in South Lancashire', in Wilson, John, H. (2009), *King Cotton - a tribute to Douglas Farnie.*

Lawton, G.O. (1979), Northwich Hundred Poll Tax, 1660, and Hearth Tax, 1664, *Record Society of Lancashire and Cheshire*, vol cxix.

Lee, Clive H. (1972), *A Cotton Enterprise 1795 –1840; a history of McConnel and Kennedy.*

Lewis, Peta (1986), "William Lee's Stocking Frame; Technical Evolution and Economic Viability 1589 – 1750", *Textile History* 17/2, 1986, pp 129 – 148.

Lowe, N. (1972), 'The Lancashire textile industry in the sixteenth century', *Chetham Society*, 3rd Series, vol. 20.

Maddison, Angus (2007), *Contours of the World Economy, 1 - 2030 AD*.

Martines, L. (1980), *Power and Imagination: city states in Renaissance Italy* (Yale Univ. Press).

Mather, R. (1780) (Anon.), *Impartial Representation of the case of the poor cotton spinners in Lancashire*, Manchester, 1780, reprinted in *Labour disputes in the early days of the Industrial Revolution*, Arno Press, New York, 1972.

Mazzaoui, M. F. (1981), *The Italian cotton industry in the later Middle Ages, 1100-1600*.

Meisenzahl, R., & Mokyr, Joel (2011), "Is Education Policy Innovation Policy", VoxEU.org/index, 13 June.

Millard, A.M. (1956), *Analysis of port books 1558-1640*, compiled 1950-9, bound typescript, Brit. Lib. & Univ. of London PhD thesis.

Mokyr, Joel (1990), *The Lever of Riches: Technological Creativity and Economic Progress*.

Mokyr, Joel (2009), *The Enlightened Economy – an Economic History of Britain 1700 – 1850*, Yale Univ. Press.

Montgomery, Florence M, (1984), *Textiles in America* (New York).

Mowl, Tim & Earnshaw, Brian (1995), *Architecture without Kings: the Rise of Puritan Classicism under Cromwell*.

Musson, Albert E. & Robinson, Eric (1969), *Science and Technology in the Industrial Revolution,* ch. 13.

Ogden, James, (1783), *Manchester – a hundred years ago*, ed. William E.A. Axon., originally pub.1783, reprinted 1887 & 1968.

Ogilvie, S. (1997), *State corporatism and proto-industry – the Wurtemberg Black Forest, 1580-1797.*

Oxford Archaeology North, vol 13 (2007), *A & G Murray and the cotton mills of Ancoats*.

Paas, M.W. (1979), *Population change, labour supply and agriculture in Augsburg, 1480-1618* (New York).

Pardi, G. (1896), *Il Catasto d'Orvieto dell'anno 1292* (Perugia) and in *Bollettino della Regia Deputazione di Storie Patria per l'Umbria*, t.2 (Perugia), pp 225-318.

Phillips, Colin B. & Smith, John H. (1994), *Lancashire and Cheshire from 1540.*

Phillips, Kevin (1999), *The Cousins' Wars: Religion, politics and the triumph of Anglo-America* (New York).

Porter, Stephen (1994), *Destruction in the English Civil Wars* (Dover, New Haven).

Power, Michael (2000), 'Creating a Port: Liverpool 1695 -1715' in *Transactions of the Historic Society of Lancashire & Cheshire,* vol 149.

Pullan, Brian (1973), *A history of Early Renaissance Italy from the mid-thirteenth to the mid-fifteenth century.*

Radelet, Steven (2010), *Emerging Africa*, (Washington DC Centre for Global Development).

Riello, Georgio and Parthasarathi, Prasannan (2009), *The Spinning world, Global History of cotton textiles 1200 – 1850.*

Roberts, E. (1998)(ed.) *A History of Linen in the North-west.*

Robisheaux, T. (1989), *Rural society and the search for order in Early Modern Germany.*

Rollison, David (2011), *Community, Country and Commonwealth.*

Rose, Arthur.G. (1963-4), "Early Cotton Riots in Lancashire 1769 – 1779", *Transactions of the Lancashire & Cheshire Antiquarian Society*, vol. 73-4.

Scott, Tom (1986), *Freiburg and the Breisgau.*

Scott, Tom (2001), 'Town and country in Germany, 1350-1600' in Epstein, S.R. (ed.) *Town and country in Europe.*

Scott, Tom (2002), 'German Peasants' War and the "Crisis of Feudalism" ', *Journal of Early Modern History*, 6, 3.

Scott, Tom, & Scribner, B. (1991), (eds) *The German Peasants' War; a history in documents* (New Jersey).

Sella, Domenico (1979) *Crisis and Continuity*, (Harvard Univ Press).

Smith, Adam, (1776), *Wealth of Nations*, ed. Connan, E., Methuen, London, 1904, ebook on Library of Economics and Liberty (www.econlib.org)

Spufford, Margaret (1974), *Contrasting communities: English villagers in the 16th and 17th centuries.*

Spufford, P. (1986), *Handbook of medieval exchange*, RHS Guide No 13.

Sreenivasan, G.P. (2004), *The peasants of Ottobeuren, 1486-1726.*

Swain, J.T. (1986), *Industry before the Industrial Revolution. North-east Lancashire c. 1500 – 1640*, Chetham Society, 3rd Series, vol. 32.

Tait, J. (1924), *Taxation in Salford Hundred 1524 – 1802*, Chetham Society, New Series, vol. 83.

Thick, Malcolm (1998), *The Neat House Gardens: Early Market gardening around London.*

Tupling, G.H. (1927), *The economic history of Rossendale*, Chetham Society, New Series, Vol. 86.

Unwin, George (1968), *Samuel Oldknow and the Arkwrights.*

Wadsworth, Alfred, & Mann, Julia de L. (1931), *The Cotton Trade and Industrial Lancashire 1600 – 1780.*

Waley, D. (1969), *The Italian City-republics.*

Waley, D. (1991), *Siena and the Sienese in the thirteenth century.*

Watson, Andrew M. (1983), *Agricultural Innovation in the early Islamic World.*

Willan (1936), *River Navigation in England* 1600 - 1750.

Willan, T.S. (1955), 'Some aspects of English trade in the Levant in the sixteenth century', *Economic History Review*, 2nd Series, LXX.

Withersby, J.P. (1998), *Linen Men*, MA Thesis 9011, Univ. of Liverpool.

Wood, A.C. (1933), *History of the Levant Company.*

www.ectonvillage.co.uk/bfranklin.html.

www.stg.brown.edu/projects/catasto. www.disc.wisc.edu/catasto.

Wyke, John (1978), *Catalogue 1758-82*, printed for Wintherthur Museum by Univ. of Virginia Press, Charlottesville.

Zmora, H. (1997), *State and nobility in early modern Germany, 1440-1567*.